# GOD

## *The Oldest Question*

---

A FRESH LOOK AT BELIEF
AND UNBELIEF—
AND WHY THE CHOICE MATTERS

WILLIAM J. O'MALLEY

LOYOLAPRESS.

3441 N. ASHLAND AVENUE
CHICAGO, ILLINOIS 60657

Scripture quotations marked TEV are from the Today's English Version—Second Edition © 1992 by American Bible Society. Used by permission.

*Interior design by Lisa Buckley*

**Library of Congress Cataloging-in-Publication Data**
O'Malley, William J.
        God : the oldest question / William J. O'Malley.
                p. cm.
        Includes bibliographical references.
        ISBN 0-8294-1515-7 (pbk.)
            1. God. 2. Faith. I. Title.

BT102 .O437 2000
231—dc21

                                        00-025507
                                        CIP

Printed in the United States of America
        03  04  Bang  10  9  8  7  6  5  4

# GOD

*The Oldest Question*

———

*This book is for*

*Dick McCurdy, S.J., and Stan O'Konsky, S.J.,*

*my wise* daimons

# CONTENTS

# I

## TO THE SEEKER

Yet all experience is an arch wherethrough
Gleams that untraveled world, whose margin fades
For ever and for ever when I move.
How dull it is to pause, to make an end,
To rust unburnished, not to shine in use!
As though to breathe were life!

—ALFRED, LORD TENNYSON, "ULYSSES"

Human beings are the only creatures we know who are incomplete. Rocks will never be more or less flinty; carrots will never be more or less vegetable; cows will never be more or less bovine. But humans are free to be more—or less—human. Witness the vast spectrum that separates Dr. Josef Mengele from Dr. Albert Schweitzer.

The human heart is restless. "Is that all there is?" There has to be more. Some assuage this human hunger by grasping for more and more money, fame, sex, power. The evidence—Elvis Presley, Marilyn Monroe, Howard Hughes, and a host of others who "had it all" and yet killed themselves—proves unarguably that more "things" leave us still unsatisfied. Nonetheless, my thirty-five years' experience with young people shows that every single one of them resolutely believes that "things" can, and almost surely will, make them happy. I wish them luck in their ill-fated dreams.

To be fully human is to seek. We seek not just for food or facts, not just for the lay of the land or hints of danger (the alertness we share with other animals), but also for meaning. We want a purpose, a motive—however ill-focused—to go on. The alternative to Ulysses' quest is Macbeth's existentialist cry of anguish:

> Tomorrow, and tomorrow, and tomorrow
> Creeps in this petty pace from day to day
> To the last syllable of recorded time;
> And all our yesterdays have lighted fools
> The way to dusty death. . . . [Life] is a tale
> Told by an idiot, full of sound and fury,
> Signifying nothing.

Why do human beings have a preference for truth rather than error? for knowledge rather than ignorance? for rationality rather than relativism? for order and justice rather than chaos and anarchy? Where do those inner compasses come from?

Perhaps they come from some Higher Power who (or which) also values truth, knowledge, rationality, order, and justice. Many argue the contrary—that our approval of moral goodness came accidentally as a result of evolution, in which survival went to the fittest. But survival of the fittest teaches that nice guys finish last—the opposite of what we want to believe. Perhaps strange aliens arrived on earth one day and fused into a simian brain some neural chip that at least invites us to larger lives. But we sure didn't get that urge from King Kong.

Ironically, human restlessness is a search for rest. We want peace of soul, the feeling of being "at home" with who we are and where we are within the whole web of connections with our fellow humans and with our environment to the uttermost reaches of human meaning. Again ironically, the pursuit of happiness is not the pursuit of a quiescent goal—a South Seas island where all our needs are satiated. We can't remain human without the seeking. Therefore, whatever happiness means must encompass both the restlessness and the peace. Happiness is a side effect of the quest; the human goal is the pursuit itself!

What we seek is the serenity of the tightrope walker, the cancer-ward nurse, the person who defuses bombs; we seek tranquillity in the heart of the hurricane. As with Ulysses, in the going we're already "there."

Most human beings have focused the source of meaning in an Entity variously referred to as the gods, Brahman, the Uncaused First Cause, Yahweh, Ahura Mazda, Allah, Manitou. People saw the order and predictability of the stars and the seasons and concluded that some Mind must be behind their design. They were convinced of an Entity who is purposeful and who gives purpose to all that is—to the beauty and power of nature, to the unexpected challenges and to the moments of grace, to the emergence of life and to its cessation. Since the dawn of reason, most humans have believed in a dimension to human life beyond the here-and-now, commonsense, everyday world. For that reason, only human animals respectfully dispose of their dead.

Books that map out the quest for this Ultimate Reality, this Mind Behind It All, mostly suggest beginning by reading the Bible, communing with nature, or opening the inner self in solitude to the Energy behind everything. I propose that you start even before that—with an acknowledgment of your own inner need for God (whatever that Meaning-Provider might turn out to be). Even atheists have an idea of God. Perhaps there is no Entity outside our minds to validate the idea of God, but there is within each of us a God-sized hunger no earthly entity can satisfy. If in fact there is no Being to corroborate our God-idea, we are left with yet another question: Why are we the only species cursed with a hunger for a food that doesn't exist?

Augustine said, "Our hearts are restless till they rest in Thee." The purpose of this book is to discover if Augustine was right.

## OBSTACLES

The greatest obstacle in the search for God is indifference, what George Eliot called "unreflecting egotism." Many of us tend to be self-preoccupied and complacent: "I can take care of myself." That uncritical smugness can last quite some time, perhaps for years, but there will almost certainly come the unexpected ambush when our world seems to fall apart and our narcissism begins to crack. Still, even an omnipotent God can't penetrate the defenses of the self-absorbed, closed-fisted, closed-hearted, closed-minded, unreflective egotist. According to the Beatitudes (unless their source was a charlatan or a madman), God is most readily available to the empty-handed.

However, most people who pick up this book have legitimate questions. They do not belong to the unlettered, unquestioning masses who bowed slavishly at any totem the shaman erected or who flocked dutifully to worship in temple or chapel or mosque. Is it possible that God and all things religious and theological are no more than an atavistic throwback, like the jitters from passing a graveyard or the fear of walking under a ladder or stepping on a crack in the sidewalk? Could it be that, all along, God was merely a way of keeping us in line, like Santa Claus ("You better watch out; you better not cry")? Anyone with a reasonably sophisticated education faces genuine obstacles to accepting an all-powerful, all-knowing, all-competent Entity whom no one has ever seen. For many well-read, thoughtful people, the need for God as an explanation for anything keeps diminishing as science progresses. Atheist humanism makes a strong case against a God who interferes with human autonomy and nullifies the value of human achievements.

Most tellingly, the unquestionable existence of physical and moral evil offers strong evidence against a provident God who wants the best for each of us. In the face of the suffering of innocent children, one is tempted to believe that if there is a God responsible for everything, God is a sadist.

Yet another obstacle to thinking about an Entity more important than all others is the way we have trivialized God and any other transcendent reality in our all-pervasive, bubblegum-for-the-mind media. God is George Burns; angels are Della Reese and Roma Downey; Satan is Al Pacino. We reincarnate the tremendous forces our ancestors believed in into our own bland image. TV and movies have numbed us to horror. Newspaper stories of child rape, child murder, children bloat-bellied and starving have become mere background noise. We speak of "dysfunctional behavior" rather than "sin." Young people who are spineless and promiscuous are really "high spirited." We are hesitant to condemn anything as objectively evil lest we appear closed minded or judgmental. For most of the world's history, the greatest talents of any society were focused on glorifying the Ultimate Reality; now they're focused on glorifying automobiles and toilet-bowl cleaners. Woody Allen nailed it: "Not only is God dead, but try to get a plumber on a weekend."

Finally, to be perfectly honest, as G. K. Chesterton said, "the greatest obstacle to Christianity is Christians." Those of us in the dwindling number who remember the admittedly triumphalist church before Vatican II miss the surge of energy that supported our flagging faith with soaring Gregorian chants, Tenebrae, and even the full-throated response to "Holy God, We Praise Thy Name." We even mourn the near-total disappearance of hellfire-and-brimstone sermons, which at least made our souls important enough to care about. We balk at "Christianity Lite." When Clare Boothe Luce was considering converting to Catholicism, she said she used to study Catholics and say to herself, "You say you have the truth. Well, the truth should set you free, give you joy. Can I *see* your freedom? Can I *feel* your joy?" Nifty questions.

I have my work cut out for me.

## THE MEANING OF RELIGIOUS FAITH

Most people probably equate religion with going to church. Not really true. There have been many saints (Albert Camus, for instance) who never went to church. There are not a few (though fewer than the disaffected would claim) who attend worship religiously but are more mean spirited, tough hearted, and hypocritical than most renegades from formal religion.

The Latin root of *religion* is *religare,* "to bind fast." Therefore, genuine religion is a *connection* to the Ultimate Reality and, by extension, to one's fellow worshipers. If there is no real, felt connection to either, but merely pro forma endurance of a ritual, there is no religion. Simple as that. Worshipers must look into their own hearts, inaccessible to outside scrutiny or judgment, and assess for themselves whether theirs is real religion.

For years, my Western bias led me to believe that to be legitimate, the connection had to be person-to-Person. I thought that unless the Deity was a someone and not just a force, the word *religion* was misused. Now I am not as sure as I was. Some Hindus and Buddhists believe Brahman to be personal; others do not and yet feel a personal connection to a Power, a transcendent Energy. Who am I to say that theirs is not genuine religion? We will discuss this question when we consider insights into the transcendent from the viewpoint of Eastern thinkers.

Still, when called upon to give a homily at the funeral of a seventeen-year-old suicide victim (as I have been more often than I'd have liked), I know that my listeners need something more accessible than the Ineffable Oversoul or the Uncaused First Cause, much less the laws of physics.

Almost everyone whom I've asked what the meaning of faith is has an explanation that is light-years from the truth. They call it "a blind leap in the dark." I have no idea whence that crackbrained notion arose, but I know it's commonplace and nearly ineradicable. A blind leap in the dark is sheer idiocy. It's like hearing a description of your roommate's sister and saying, "OK, I'll marry her." It's like giving five grand for an acre of land in Florida you've never seen. It's the order "Just have faith!" or, worse, "Because I said so!" from a parent who's been demonstrably wrong before. Place my trust in a God you've never even introduced me to? Almost as bad, the *Catechism of the Catholic Church* at least three times equates faith with obedience; in other words, "Just bring all your questions to us, and you can have faith that we'll give you the final answers." Having had three years of philosophy and four years of theology (in Latin), most of which I have mercifully forgotten, I'm a little more skeptical than that. And being for the last thirty-six years one of those officials who are supposed to have all those answers, I am even less sanguine.

Consider the meaning of faith involved in any commitment other than a religious one—a marriage, a career, a business partnership. A genuine act of faith in these matters is neither a blind leap in the dark (which is irrational) nor an assent with absolute certitude (which is impossible). Faith is neither—and both. (It's called the law of complementarity, which we will see much more of later.) Faith is a *calculated risk*. You examine the evidence as honestly as you can, but no matter how scrupulous your research, there's still a possibility you're wrong. That's where the risk comes in. A husband and a wife don't *know* that their marriage will work out; they're *betting* on it. The more careful the calculation, the less the risk. I don't know that God exists, but I've examined the evidence for and against God more than most people, and I'm reasonably sure there is a higher probability for a Mind Behind It All than for its absence. I've bet my life on it.

As we shall see, the result of the faith choice is far more important than the evidence that motivated the leap.

Thomas the Apostle was a saint—and a doubter: "I want *evidence*. It may not be utterly conclusive, but I want more than a mere 'Trust me' before I join hands with you and leap off a cliff." There is a sanctity in doubt that churches have too long belittled, if not scorned. Doubt in your mind is like a pain in your body, a signal that everything isn't as serene as you thought, that something in your certitudes rings false and needs tinkering. The great sin is certitude; the great virtue is doubt. "I believe. Help my unbelief."

## THE MEANING OF SCIENTIFIC PROOF

People wavering between belief and unbelief often wish that someone could give them scientific proof about God, one way or the other. They want proof as beyond dispute as the fact that we will all die and that dropped bricks will go down. We trust science because of its results. We want the same undeniable results from religion: "If you show me a miracle, I'll believe. If God answers my prayers, I'll believe." We forget that if we'd been standing next to Jesus when he turned water into wine, our first natural reaction would have been, "How the hell did you do that? It defies the laws of chemistry." And if he had said, "It's really rather easy. You see, I'm God," we would have replied, "So long, Jesus." We forget too that when God doesn't answer our prayers, "No" is, in fact, an answer.

The desire for such irrefutable proof about God comes from a rather naive view of science. What scientists accept as proof is not certitude but a high degree of *probability;* it is acceptance (for the moment) of a conclusion with no reasonable doubt. We've known since before 1932, when Werner Heisenberg won the Nobel Prize in physics, that we can be pretty sure of an electron's location or velocity—but not both at the same time, since locating the electron changes its velocity. Scientific proof is about as reliable as planning a wedding in July rather than in November or predicting election results when the majority of the polls haven't closed yet or knowing that two-thirds of American males will reach their seventies—without knowing whether one is in the two-thirds or the one-third. *Scientific proof* usually means "fairly reliable."

The major difference between scientific conclusions and religious conclusions is that for the most part, scientific experiments are *public;* that is, anyone with sufficient expertise can see them, understand them, and reproduce them. By contrast, religious conclusions often rest on evidence and experiences that are *private;* that is, they occur within an individual and are not easily reproduced, even by someone of goodwill and certainly not by someone skeptical of any reality that is not physical. In a strictly rational inquiry, personal, private encounters with God or any transcendent reality are inadmissible evidence.

However, that exclusion of private evidence is highly reductionist—the same sort of simplism that reduces human beings to rational animals, as if we were no more than apes with implanted computers. It suggests that there are no genuine and undeniable human experiences *not* rooted in either the body or the brain (both of which we share with other animals). Selfless love, honor, loyalty, and commitment are not strictly rational, but they are in no way irrational, just as getting married and deciding to have children are neither totally logical nor sheerly biological decisions. Entrusting a secret to a friend is both rational and nonrational: a calculated risk.

There is solid evidence to vindicate our right to affirm God's existence. This is not a reproducible demonstration but an accumulation of enough reliable evidence to show that God's existence is at least defensible.

The transcendent conviction has been accumulating far longer and from a far wider segment of the human population than what science has accumulated. This segment includes not only superstitious savages and little old ladies with plastic rosaries but also such unquestioned worthies as Plato, Aristotle, the Buddha, Jesus, Saul of Tarsus (a religious persecutor), Augustine, Aquinas, Galileo, Thomas More, Erasmus, Luther, Newman, C. S. Lewis, Dorothy Sayers, Simone Weil, Edith Stein, and Dorothy Day. None of them easily hoodwinked.

In the course of these pages we will deal with a great many "head trip" attacks and defenses of belief, but religion's only sure proof (unsusceptible to scientific scrutiny) is the way honest belief and the "connection" change people's everyday lives. Does belief make them wiser, more courageous, more concerned? In all these wildly disparate and often antagonistic groups of believers, their faith has allowed them placidly to accept the unacceptable, to forgive the unforgivable, to love the unlikable. Except for some privileged persons and occasions, their testimony to the transcendent (like any genuine love) is remarkably undramatic: ordinary lives lived in an extraordinary way. Surely it has nothing to do with the airless abstractions I dealt with in four years of theology.

In fact, the only way to an irrefutable answer to the God questions is precisely to leave behind the search for rational evidence *about* God and go in search *of* God. All this book attempts is some kind of encouragement to show that such a search is worth the effort.

Jacob wrestled with God; in fact, that's what his name means. Anyone who has experienced God, wrestled with God, cursed God can live with biblical inconsistencies and even with baptized (or ordained) hypocrites and fools. When you've been ravished by God, what seemed like the wrath of God *is* the love of God, assessed by a fool.

## THE LIMITS OF LANGUAGE

A dozen years ago, more than a bit against my will, I attended a retreat preached by a world-famous Indian Jesuit whose opening remarks were something to the effect of "You think you know about God. You don't know anything about God. All you believe about God is false." Since most of the audience were women and men vowed to poverty, chastity, and obedience for thirty years or more, the effect was electric. Which I suspect is precisely what he wanted. I could understand why he refused to let anyone tape-record his remarks. When he asked for questions, I overcame my fabled shyness and asked, "Do you mean that what we say about God is only remotely, remotely true? Or are you saying that anything we say about God is utterly false?" And his reply was, "Utterly false. Can you describe green to a blind man?" And I responded that of course I could: "Green is like chomping a bunch of mint leaves and sucking the juice. And red is like hot cinnamon candy on your tongue. That's not what they are, but it's better than nothing." He scoffed at that, and when others raised the same objection, he said, "That's like Bill's problem. We'll get back to Bill's problem later." Needless to say, I shook the dust from my feet and made that retreat alone with the God I've been trying to cope with for half a century.

All analogies limp; when it comes to God they scarcely crawl, like trying to explain orgasm (which is real) to a ten-year-old. But to focus on their inadequacy rather than on the small light they can shed on a mystery is like focusing on Stephen Hawking's body rather than on his mind (to use an analogy).

Words are more than fairly reliable when they are univocal—*oak, Ford, dandruff*—though each object that clusters around those words remains unique. But it takes a bit of mental juggling when words are equivocal: *Ring* could be a place for a boxing match, a symbol of marriage, the sound of a bell, the soap scum around a bathtub. We use *love* for all kinds of different relationships: pizza, my dog, my mother, affection, lust. When we say, "I'd love to bash that guy's head in," we've gone beyond a legitimate use of the word. Analogical use of words applies them to two objects partly in the same sense but partly in a different sense. For instance, you've never met Alfie and know nothing about him. "Well, Alfie's a pig." Some things you can truly say about both Alfie and pigs (fat, sloppy, coarse, hairy, unkempt), but some things you can't (curly tail, stove-plate snout, trotters). Nonetheless, the things you can legitimately say about both give you at least a less hazy idea about something you didn't know anything at all about before.

As we'll see later, analogy is the only way we can deal with many truths, like subatomic particles, which don't really act the way things do in the commonsense world. If you ran into a wall, for instance, you'd expect to get flattened against it. But it's quite likely that an electron racing toward the same wall would simply appear on the other side without leaving a hole behind it. If you could shoot an electron from an electron "gun" through a barrier with two holes, it might go through both holes at once—since sometimes electrons act like pellets and at other times like waves. Well, which is it? Uh, both. And, uh, neither. Complementarity again. The contraries together explain this barely known entity better than either one alone—just as with male/female, angel/savage, science/religion.

> There are more things in heaven and earth, Horatio,
> than are dreamt of in your philosophy.

If God exists, there's nobody else in God's class. God is unutterably "other." We can't use the words *person* or *know* or *love*—or even *exist*—about God in anything remotely like the way we are persons who know, love, and exist. This limitation of language gives rise to the problem of anthropomorphism, applying to God the meanings of words as they apply to us—the only beings of whom we have firsthand knowledge. This is trying to understand God as if God were patterned on us rather than the other way around. "If God can see the future and knows when I'm going to sin, why can't he stop me?" God doesn't *fore*see the future; God *sees* it.

Nonetheless, if we are made in the image of God, we actually can find out something about this Mind Behind It All by looking at ourselves, just as we can better understand the personalities of Michelangelo and Picasso and Monet by looking at their work. God, if God exists, is not anthropomorphic, but we human beings are *theo*morphic. When we consider elements in human nature that separate us from other animals, we can get some remote insight into God.

The first problem in beginning to understand God is with the limitations of our intelligence. We have the unwitting conviction that if something is there, we should see it, that if something is explained, we should understand it. If we can't understand it (like the inner workings of the atom), then it's not worth bothering about. This reaction is naive. You can't see, smell, touch, or taste most of the realities in your room: radio waves, muons, gluons, quarks, neutrinos. You can't see most of the light spectrum. The rock that skins your knee isn't really rock-solid but a cloud of atoms—and most of it is empty space. If all those particles were packed together, the rock would have a billionth of the bulk apparent to your senses.

The second problem is with God—not that God is unintelligible, but that God (if God exists) is an *excess* of intelligibility. Take a homely example: I love books, but when I go into a huge bookstore like Borders or Barnes & Noble or The Strand, I'm overwhelmed—like a diabetic in a candy store. It's the same with God; there's just too much to take in. And God is perfect (though Langston Hughes described God poetically saying, "I'm lonely. I'll make me a world"). God can't be lonely. Nor, despite what well-meaning parents and grade-school teachers say, can our sins hurt God or make God cry. That's sheer anthropomorphism, making God in our image rather than vice versa. Not legitimate analogies.

In religion or in science, we have to develop a tolerance for ambiguity; we need genuine open-mindedness, without preconceptions, hidden agendas, vested interests—whether theist or atheist.

The laws of science and the laws of divine behavior are not quite ironbound. Science, for instance, declares that there can be no entity faster than light. But science delights in playing "what if." What if there were a reality faster than light? It would be moving so fast that it would be everywhere at once. Like God. It would be so superenergized that it would be at rest. Like God. Couple that with God's quite unscientific answer to Moses' request to know God's name, God's function: "I am who am." I Am is the pool of existence out of which everything that is draws its "is," the transcendent Energy who powers all you see. Seen in that way, the two approaches—science and religion— seem much more complementary. Truth is greater than facts.

One final and perhaps peripheral note on the limits of language regarding God is the pronoun problem. I will make every effort in these pages to use inclusive language, but when it comes to God, I balk. We're talking about someone who's been my Friend/Antagonist for over sixty-five years. I find it impossible to treat such a person as if it had suddenly become a hermaphrodite. I know I skirt anthropomorphism here; I also know that—being outside time and space—God has no genitals, no white beard, and thus is not male. I do believe that the Holy Spirit is a feminine principle within God, just as the book of Wisdom pictures her. But in my experience, God is—in the sense of Carl Jung—far more masculine (challenging, rational, decisive, unbending) than feminine (cherishing, enfolding, mothering, consoling). Again in my experience, if God is a "she," God is one damn tough cookie.

The pronoun problem focused itself while I was proofreading another book I wrote. The editor—a woman—called and said she didn't know how to avoid the pronoun problem when I talked about it being OK to get angry at God. I had written something like "Take God out for a walk. Call him every rotten name you can think of. Then forgive him, for all the good times, because there surely have been more good times with him than bad times." In that particular situation, there was no way she could change it to "Call him/her every rotten name you can think of." All the force of forgiving a Friend who's betrayed your trust would be lost in service of political correctness. The "he" analogy crawls, but it is the only way I can approach the outskirts of God.

## MYSTERY

*Detective mystery* is a misuse of the term. A whodunit isn't a mystery; it's a problem, exactly like a high school math problem or experiment. Before the publisher will accept the detective story, she and the author have to know how the problem resolves itself. High school lab books don't describe experiments in the sense of a tentative procedure to discover something unknown or test a principle. It's a recipe, and if you don't mess up, it will end predictably.

On the contrary, a mystery is open ended; you're never going to nail it down. Nor is God the only mystery. Love, what lies beyond death, the reasons for the seventeen-year-old's suicide, the prosperity of the cynical, the failure of the good-souled, why this woman and man have managed to hold together a marriage for fifty years—all are unfathomable. The fascination of genuine mystery is not that it baffles but that it opens up, like a lotus. It invites exploration, but it defies conquest.

Hard-nosed rationalism insists that whatever *is* can be understood. This claim is as credulous as believing that if there is a murderer, he or she will surely be found. We crave closure, but in so many of life's very real puzzlements, closure is impossible.

The first step on the quest for God is to admit (in both senses: acknowledge and welcome) at least the possibility of the transcendent, a dimension to our lives that invites exploration and defies conquest. In the opening sentence of *Cosmos,* Carl Sagan said, "The Cosmos is all that is or ever was or ever will be." In one inaugural sentence, he closed the question: There *cannot* be any reality beyond our commonsense world. Coming from such a rightly renowned scientist, that strikes me as manifestly unscientific. The genial atheist from Cornell joined the dour fathers of the Inquisition who threatened to burn Galileo because the sun *cannot* be the center of the solar system. Denying that anything can exist (other than squared circles or dehydrated water) is as arrogant as denying that black holes can exist or that there could be a planet on which unicorns gambol. I'd like to visit a planet like that.

### THE QUEST

We will begin the search for clues to God in what might seem an odd place: among the atheists. For one thing, they obviously deserve a say in the question. For another, any theist who has never examined the legitimate contrary arguments doesn't really embrace theism freely. If two roads diverge in a yellow wood, and you are utterly unaware that one exists, you take the only road you believe available. Just as we saw that there are many geniuses who embraced theism, there are also more than a few geniuses who embraced atheism: Nietzsche, David Hume, Bertrand Russell, Alfred North Whitehead, Jean-Paul Sartre, Simone de Beauvoir. Stephen Hawking, although he seems obsessed with God, balks at either acceptance or denial. Moreover, it is wise to understand what our lives would be like if we could shed ourselves of the transcendent crutch and live with an atheist denial in a world without God, guilt, or grace.

After looking at the atheists, we will explore hints about a Mind Behind It All revealed in numinous experiences. These are moments when we get what my friend Michael Kelly calls "epiphanal goose bumps": a mountain at dawn, a storm-ravaged seacoast, a baby's fingers curling around your pinky—moments when we say, "Wow!" or "Oh, my God!" That response, a theist would say, is eminently proper, giving praise to the Artist for his work. Conversely, an atheist would say that such responses are merely a shock to the senses, given significance internally by the subject rather than resulting from any provable objective presence that triggers them.

In the fourth chapter, we will explore what we can learn about the Mind Behind It All from the complexities and simplicities of science, what we can understand about that Mind from the philosophers—without reference to any religion at all. We can learn, for instance, that if there is a God, God is interested in not only order (the design of the universe) but also surprise (the uniqueness of every snowflake).

But we cannot derive from reason alone—from nature, from science, from effect-to-cause philosophy—that God is personal, provident, concerned. We can discover those insights only from revelation, encounters with God by heroic souls and by ordinary souls. Therefore, we will next consider the insights into the transcendent in Eastern thought—a mind-set not readily accessible to someone trained in the rigid logic of the Greek-Hebrew West. Then we will consider insights from the religions rooted in Abraham and Moses: Judaism, Christianity, and Islam. After that, we will ponder what we can find out about the nature and personality of God from the man and the message of Jesus—not Christianity as a doctrinal system, but the root person out of whom Christianity emerged.

Finally, we will seek clues about God in much homelier places—in silent receptivity, in other people, in suffering—where the God question is no longer academic.

I do believe that we can find God, apprehend God. Not physically see, hear, or touch. Not comprehend, fathom, fully understand. But we can contact God, engage God person-to-Person. If God exists, God is—literally—everywhere, in ecstasy and in bereavement, in creating and in rebuilding, in community and in solitude. The Baal Shem Tov, founder of Hasidism, said that when God returned to heaven after creating, he celebrated by throwing radiant sparks of light into the air, showering the earth. And the sparks embedded themselves in every rock and tree and in every human heart. Though our eyes are benighted, we set off in a quest for that Light.

## 2

## THE PATH TO GOD
## THROUGH ATHEISM

"Now, what I want is Facts," [says Mr. Gradgrind
to the terrified pupils of the school he subsidizes].
"Teach these boys and girls nothing but Facts. Facts
alone are wanted in life. Plant nothing else, and
root out everything else. You can only form the
minds of reasoning animals upon Facts: nothing else
will ever be of any service to them. . . . Stick to the
Facts, sir!"

—CHARLES DICKENS, *HARD TIMES*

Ayear before my ordination as a priest, I was literally
ready to commit suicide. I had spent six years studying scholas-
tic philosophy and theology—in Latin. Almost none of it
seemed to have any reference whatever to what people would
expect from a good priest or even from an educated human
being. That year, the preeminent American theologian John
Courtney Murray was teaching us a Latin Trinity text by the
preeminent Canadian theologian Bernard Lonergan—in
Latin. To me, it was like learning celestial calculus in Japanese.
Scripture courses had stripped away my innocent, unquestionable, pre–Vatican II peasant faith and left not much more than
habit in its place. My grades in the once-a-year exams (oral,
in Latin) were not just embarrassing but humiliating: at best
*mediocritas;* at worst, *non superat mediocritatem* ("He doesn't

achieve even mediocrity"). What's more, we lived in an all-male community of about 250, sequestered in the woods: an occasional movie but no radio or TV. We were all in our early thirties, when the hormones show little mercy and no signs of abating. According to my psychiatrist, who had visited there before I knew him, it was sensual deprivation worthy of a gulag.

Since I had always based my worth on hard work and an assurance of good grades, my self-esteem could be reckoned only in negative numbers. More than once, I told my spiritual father that I felt like a bucket of scum. I couldn't escape the temptation to believe that I had been colossally hoaxed for my entire life. A Jewish carpenter was the embodiment of God? And his entire claim was based on the conviction of his rising from the dead—an event that nobody witnessed? And the God who created everything was one God yet also three? And I was engaged in this mind-withering educational process in order to make myself worthy to call God out of . . . wherever, into a wafer of bread and an ounce of wine? And to be able to serve this all-powerful, all-knowing, all-loving (and sublimely silent and unforthcoming) God in the best way possible, I had surrendered sex, money, and independence not just temporarily but forever? Right.

Yet something held me back from killing myself—or, less dramatically, from leaving the Society of Jesus after an investment of twelve years and perhaps even leaving a church that had always and without question been the rock on which rested everything I believed true. So I decided to do what my training and my own never-questioned convictions had forbidden me to do. I decided to give atheists a chance to shatter my naïveté. I wanted them to carpet bomb the City of God and allow me to start over, building from scratch using only what I knew to be true. I wanted what Descartes wanted: "evidence so clear and distinct I have no occasion to doubt it."

As I read (especially from within my swamp of self-pity), the atheists really began to make sense, especially Albert Camus, whose bleak struggle against absurdity in his *Myth of Sisyphus* seemed exactly my own. According to the Greek myth, the gods condemned the Titan Sisyphus to roll a huge rock up a mountainside, but every time he finally accomplished the task and stood on the peak wiping the sweat from his brow, the rock rolled back down again. Sisyphus had to push the rock up the mountain again. Over and over. "Tomorrow, and tomorrow, and tomorrow creeps in this petty pace." But Camus extrapolated the myth. At some point, he said, Sisyphus must have stopped and begun to think. "Why am I doing this? And in the end, when I'm too weak to go on, I have nothing to face except annihilation at death? Why not just commit suicide and get it over with?"

Precisely my question.

As Sisyphus stood there pondering, Camus suggested, he suddenly grasped a reason to go on: stubborn pride. At that moment, he fired an arm at the indifferent universe and cried defiantly, "I won't quit!" In the ultimately meaningless struggle to succeed, Sisyphus forged his own meaning from sheer bitchery.

An atheist may not have kept me in the seminary or in the church, but he did keep me from taking a window for a door into ersatz peace. That was the first step out of my swamp.

## THE CASE FOR ATHEISM

There are really only four persuasive arguments for a world without a Mind Behind It All. The first argument—the most convincing—is the problem of pain: How can a good, knowing, all-competent God allow the anguish of innocents? The second argument—the most appealing to those with a naive idea of science—is Occam's razor: Beings are not to be postulated unless they are inescapable; to be truthful, we don't need a God. The third argument—the most abstruse—is the meaninglessness of the term *God,* which denotes an objectively unvalidated entity, like *unicorn* or *Santa.* The fourth argument is the most comforting for those with (often justifiable) complaints about organized religion: the negative consequences of belief. If we can cure ourselves of the illusion of God, we can take back our human dignity and autonomy from the hands of a tyrannical Bogeyman and an arrogant clergy.

## The Problem of Pain

The drunkard ingests his own punishment; the mean-spirited sentence themselves to empty lives; the grudge holder suffers anguish without affecting her putative exploiter in the least. They made their choices; let them live with the inevitable results. If lightning strikes a forest and levels it, we can see a purpose in that: new growth. But not when it strikes a village. Nor, as Voltaire pictured it in *Candide,* when an earthquake destroys the Lisbon cathedral while everyone is at All Saints' Day Mass. Good people perish; whores and corrupt churchmen survive. A provident God?

There is no comprehending the suffering of children. Nor decent, hardworking men and women. Nor Job. A great articulation of this injustice comes from Ivan Karamazov, who asks his brother Alyosha a bold question: If he could establish a universe with the intention of making everyone fulfilled—but the universe rested on the unmerited suffering of even one child (much less millions)—would he do it? Why would a decent God answer a selfish old lady's prayer to find her pampered Pekingese and let thousands of uncomprehending children die of slow starvation in Africa? And let us have no claptrap about "Oh, God wanted another bright flower in his garden" when innocent children die. Outside time and space, God doesn't have a garden, and God has no needs whatsoever. That's sheer anthropomorphism, not to mention mawkish sentimentality.

There are two basic kinds of evil: physical evil (hurricanes, cancer, death itself) and moral evil (rape, murder, indiscriminate bombing).

Physical evil can't be attributed to any human perversity or wickedness. Only the simple would say that in each specific case, God steps in and personally zaps this one with dandruff and that one with arthritis. But there is no escaping the truth that if God is responsible for this universe, God is ultimately responsible for creating a situation in which such unmerited suffering can occur. As Nickles, the cynic of Archibald MacLeish's *J. B.,* puts it, "If God is God, he is not good. If God is good, he is not God." In other words, if the One we call God is truly in charge, his tolerance of unmerited suffering proves that he is not good. Conversely, if the One we call God is truly good, then he couldn't possibly be in charge of such topsy-turvy sadism.

Moral evil is rooted in twisted humanity, what a simpler age called "original sin." A more sophisticated time says that moral evil is the residue of the animal in us: narcissism and inertia, the self-absorption that refuses to admit a mistake and the refusal to change, the reptilian brain stem freely left unconnected to the cerebral cortex. No matter what that perversity's source, the effects are evident from the first third of any tabloid newspaper: "Mother Slays Infant, Then Self," "Two Students Blow Up School with Pipe Bombs," "Hundreds of Albanian Children Killed by Mistake." Again, God did not step in and manipulate so many people to do evil to others, but God is ultimately responsible for giving freedom to an inadequately evolved tribe of apes.

## Occam's Razor

In trying to explain an effect, one ought not to go beyond perfectly satisfying explanations. If I have a headache, I should first reflect that I've been sitting here staring at a computer monitor for two hours without a break. There is no need to suspect that I have a brain tumor—much less that I have offended God in some way.

Similarly, more and more, science has proven that it can explain the universe and its human inhabitants without recourse to any cause outside physical reality. It is possible to imagine that this universe, even if it did begin with a big bang, was precipitated by a disequilibrium at the edge of some other universe. It may be that matter itself is eternal, that the Mind of God is only the laws of physics plus wishful thinking. Quite likely we are not at all responsible for our actions but are rather victims of subconscious urges and external capricious events over which we have no control. Our antisocial activities are triggered by an errant gene or an excess of sugar or faulty upbringing. Fact is a verifiable quantity; value is a man-made illusion. The sense of the supernatural some claim to experience is only a trick of the brain, and meaning is only intellectual pretense on the part of the beholder. As for the soul, there is neither need nor room to fit any nonphysical substance or properties into our theoretical account of ourselves. We are creatures of matter. Sir Cyril Bart wrote, "The chemistry of the brain generates consciousness as the liver generates bile."

Consider the infant: She is incapable of differentiating between her self and her environment; even her mother is merely an extension of her self. The whole world has become an extension of the womb, with which she has a symbiotic, self-centered relationship. Later, the sun will "follow her around," as its focus and purpose. The universe is the self; the self is the universe—as far as she is concerned from birth to death.

The truth is that human beings are merely more complex mechanisms than rocks or beets or monkeys, a belief reflected in an anonymous statement made in prewar Germany:

> The human body contains a sufficient amount of fat to make seven cakes of soap, enough iron to make a medium-sized nail, a sufficient amount of phosphorous to make two thousand match-heads, enough sulfur to rid oneself of one's fleas.

In *The Blind Watchmaker,* physicist Richard Dawkins set out explicitly to demolish the argument to God from design. Adapting the old philosophical chestnut that given enough time, a million monkeys at computers would eventually come up with all of Shakespeare, he set a chimp to come up with the line from *Hamlet* "Methinks it a little like a weasel." Starting with twenty-eight randomly generated letters and spaces, allowing mistakes every once in a while in order to get to the weasel line sheerly by chance, the chimp finally hit the perfect line after only forty-three generations, in less than an hour. Evolution, Dawkins insisted, requires only that in each generation a winner is just a hairbreadth better adapted than its peers. The only ingredients required are (1) an ability to make copies of itself, (2) occasional mistakes in the copying, and (3) some aspect of the replication that influences how likely the mistakes are to be repeated in its babies. Evolution is not a series of purposive causes and effects; it is merely a description of what actually happened.

## The Emptiness of God

Atheism insists that we don't know what we're talking about when we use the term *God.* It means nothing without a physical referent to validate it. God is a theoretical—and unobservable—explanation in the same manner as the theoretical entities like neutrinos, gravity, and instinct that scientists postulate. "Birds find their way south by instinct" is just another way of saying we don't know how they do, but they do. But controlled experiments can prove beyond a reasonable doubt that those entities are "there" in some real sense.

As we saw earlier, scientific experiments are public; they can be reproduced even by people who doubt their truth. On the contrary, numinous experiences—the sense of the presence of God—are private and nonreproducible even by open-minded skeptics. They are perhaps comforting feelings, but they are not a way to honest cognition.

Most basically, it defies reason that an all-knowing God would limit his own power by gradual and progressive evolution. If your word is sufficient to call all things into ready-made existence (as it is in Genesis), why limit your omnipotence to slow development over countless millions of years? As Carl Sagan argued, evolution doesn't support the notion of a very efficient Designer. Why waste all that time evolving species like dinosaurs and pterodactyls only to have them die out? Why tolerate human freedom—and the moral evil it causes—when this Supreme Designer could have done what B. F. Skinner tried to do: condition humans from the start to prefer righteous behavior?

## Negative Consequences of Belief

From the beginning, humans have given thanks for their good fortune to an Entity no one has ever seen, touched, or heard in any public, reproducible way. We have offered sacrifices (even human) to placate and importune a Deity who remains remarkably inaccessible to direct contact. Instead, priests, shamans, imams, ministers, rabbis, witch doctors, Pharisees, gurus, lamas, and bonzes have set themselves up as intermediaries who purport to have some privileged access to a Presence unforthcoming to ordinary folk.

What's more, these agents of an invisible and unverifiable God have achieved a control over the uninitiated that all too often usurps their ordinary common sense. In the name of Allah (masking their rulers' covetousness), countless thousands of Muslims rampaged in jihad to rape, pillage, and conquer all of North Africa, Spain, and the Near East, heedless of death, since it would be the doorway to eternal bliss. In the name of the same Deity—but with another face—the Crusades were mounted to retrieve a Holy Land that both religions claimed to be rightly theirs. In the name of a Christ whose first word was "Peace," nonconformists were sought out, tortured, and executed by the Inquisition; natives of the Americas were dispossessed of their gold, land, and lives; Galileo was forced to recant an understanding of the solar system that everyone now knows to be indisputably true; thinkers too tolerant of modern ideas like Freud's, Darwin's, and Marx's were made heretics to be scorned and stripped of credibility. Hitler preached about a Providence who decreed that those of darker-than-Aryan skin were less than human. Northern Ireland has been in murderous conflict for hundreds of years in the name of a God whom many of the participants neglect to worship.

To quote that same Christ: "By their fruits you shall know them."

## A WORLD WITHOUT GOD, GUILT, OR GRACE

There are, of course, inescapable logical consequences to ridding ourselves of the illusion of God. Along with God, we shed ourselves of the inherent, purposeful "laws" of human nature. To quote the conflicted Ivan Karamazov again, "Without God, everything is permissible." If there is in fact no Being higher than human whose manifest will and purposes can arbitrate between two equally well informed individuals or societies in dispute on any moral question, then both are right. There no longer is any objective, God-given purpose to anything. If that is the truth, as Nietzsche saw so clearly, there is only one solution to the dispute: Might makes right. Hitler believed that, and the only indication he was wrong is that he lost.

Perhaps a Divine Purposer is an illusion, but there is one reality that puts all other realities into proper perspective. Death. It is the one inescapable fact in each of our futures. Once we shake off the illusion of God, we also divest ourselves of the consolations at a wake: "Well, she's in a better life now." No, she's not in a better life; she's *not;* she stopped being real. All the struggles, failures, triumphs—all the human attributes we associate with the soul and character—are wiped out the moment we have a flat EKG, as irretrievable as a computer file lost in a power outage. *Pfft!* Gone.

There can be no genuine moral evil if humans are objectively no more than highly sophisticated animals (much less bags of chemicals and electricity). If, as any atheist would agree, only the physical is truly real and humans have no more afterlife expectancy than cattle, there really is no objective argument against the Nazi death camps. Atheists like Kai Nielsen claim that we can know right from wrong, love our children, and refrain from moral evil even without God. This is surely true, but there is no objective, rational basis for those attitudes. For entities who are, to all intents and purposes, just so much potential garbage, the difference between right and wrong is sheerly arbitrary. Love for our children is merely animal attachment to our cubs combined with sentimentality. Avoidance of moral evil is a result of mere whim and socialization.

The unsupported assertion in the first sentence of Carl Sagan's very impressive *Cosmos*—"The Cosmos is all that is or ever was or ever will be"—proves that dogmatism isn't restricted to religion. But if Sagan's assertion is true, there cannot be a God, since by definition a Creator would have to antecede its creation. Any temporary and ultimately spurious value or purpose or meaning that we can achieve must come from this limited cosmic background: time, space, and, somewhat more vaguely, human accomplishments. Those are the only yardsticks available if nothing in us transcends them.

## Time

Two-thirds of us can expect to see age seventy; the rest won't. But even for those who last to over one hundred, when the heart stops permanently, that's it. You cease to be real, like the wake of a ship. If you consider the estimated time the universe has been around, the difference between a seventeen-year life and a seventy-year life is hardly significant—except to the longer-lived person, cocooned in the deceptive importances of the everyday, who can delude himself that it is.

Sagan also showed our ultimate insignificance in another book, *The Dragons of Eden*, in which he compressed the age of the universe into a single calendar year. In that schematic, the big bang occurred the first instant of January 1, but the earth did not form until about September 14. December 24: first dino-saurs. December 31 at about 11:00 P.M.: first humans. December 31 at 11:59:59 P.M.: Renaissance in Europe. On that objectively unarguable scale, the last four hundred years have been one-sixtieth of a second. Therefore, if you lived to be one hundred, you'd live one-quarter of one-sixtieth of a second. If "the Cosmos is all that is or ever was or ever will be," the length of your days is hardly a hiccup in a hurricane.

## Space

Within the term *space,* I would include not only the portion of the earth you can conquer or own but also all the possessions you can accrue, the size of your financial holdings, the heft and girth of your body. A few of us are under five feet tall; some are six feet or taller. Inside a small room, the difference is notice-able. But put them against the Sears Tower, and it's not. Pull back even farther to an earthrise seen from the moon, and the difference is indecipherable. No wonder his contemporaries were angry at Galileo when he proved that our earth is not the center of the solar system—or for that matter the center of anything. We are certainly diminished in importance by the objective truth of our background: the cosmos.

In Lilliput, there were probably some very hefty guys and impressively portly ladies. Then Gulliver showed up. The Lilli-putians began to see their differences as insignificant contrasted to this huge intrusion on their certitudes. Think how much they would have diminished if Gulliver had managed to sneak even the largest Lilliputian into Brobdingnag, where Gulliver himself was smaller than a toy soldier. Before the two undeniable facts of the universe and death, we are utterly negligible, no matter how we persist in kidding ourselves that we have significance.

## Human Accomplishments

The accumulated value of our achievements is nonmaterial, but they are a great part of our sense of personal worth. Think of a best-case scenario. At the end of your life, you've won two Nobel Prizes, one for literature and one for curing the common cold; you've published twenty-five highly praised books; you've given the world ten superlative children—a physicist, a world-famous ballerina, a Supreme Court justice, and so on. Now place your achievements against the broader background of human history: fire, the wheel, Plato's *Dialogues,* Alexander's and Caesar's conquests, Michelangelo's art, Shakespeare's plays (all by themselves!), atomic research, space exploration. Place your twenty-five books in the Library of Congress. See your children against the one hundred thousand people who died some years ago in a Chinese earthquake. Physicists, ballerinas, judges—all were somebody's children. *Pfft!*

Against that objective background, your personal achievements look pitifully puny. And against the unfolding power of the universe, they come as close as you can get to nothing. The whole earth could explode and disappear, and the universe would hardly be the poorer.

Reading the work of true atheists is grim going. (In fact, writing this chapter has been one of the most dispiriting writing tasks I've had in a long time.) True atheists (unlike pseudoatheists such as the brainy college sophomore or the effete sophisticate) have honestly lost all hope. For true atheists, all stories come to nothing. Their essays, novels, and plays breathe a contagious world-weariness, a sexuality that sets the body on fire and leaves the spirit cold—because the spirit is a delusion. Their social theorists are pragmatic men and women for whom medical patients are interesting biological problems, soldiers are "troops" or "personnel," students are "educands." Gregor Samsa metamorphoses into a big bug, but that's all he was from the start. Matthew Arnold's lovers sit on Dover Beach and realize "we are here as on a darkling plain, swept with confused alarms of struggle and flight, where ignorant armies clash by night." Samuel Beckett's whimsically gloomy clowns know that "habit is the great deadener" because "they give birth astride of a grave. The light gleams an instant, then it's night once more." Is that all there is? Yes.

Perhaps the most chilling outcome of a world without God, guilt, or grace is the Holocaust. The Nazis gassed—or more often worked to death—eleven million people, all because they were "less than human" undesirables. A prisoner in the Dachau camp found and kept a record of how valuable each prisoner was to the Third Reich when rented out as a slave to BMW, Krupp, and Farben (RM = reichsmark).

| | |
|---|---|
| Fee received for daily rental of prisoner | 6.00 |
| Deduct cost of food | (0.60) |
| Deduct cost for use of clothes | (0.10) |
| Value of prisoner's labor per day | RM 5.30 |
| Multiply by average life span | 270 days |
| Total value of prisoner's labor | RM 1,431.00 |
| Add average proceeds from disposal of corpse (fillings, clothes, bones, valuables left with bursar) | 200.00 |
| Deduct cost of cremation | (2.00) |
| Total value of prisoner | RM 1,629.00 |

In the godless universe, that is what a human being is objectively worth. Inescapable.

## THE CASE AGAINST ATHEISM

Just like theism, atheism is an act of faith—a calculated risk. No one knows there is no God, nor can anyone prove that even the concept of God is contradictory. Just as theists have their doubts, so do atheists. *The National Review* (January 11, 1982) quoted the eminent atheist Jean-Paul Sartre just before his death: "I do not feel that I'm a product of chance, a speck of dust in the universe, but rather someone who is expected, prepared, prefigured; in short, a being whom only a Creator could have put here." David Hume and Immanuel Kant are generally credited with destroying any possible theistic evidence, yet Hume, in *Dialogues concerning Natural Religion,* spoke through his character Philo: "The cause or causes of order in the universe probably bear some remote analogy to human intelligence." And Kant in the *Critique* wrote, "Belief in a God and in another world is so interwoven with my moral sentiment that, as there is little danger of my losing the latter, there is equally little cause of fear that the former can ever be taken from me." Though hesitant about commitment one way or other about God, Stephen Hawking wrote, "It is difficult to discuss the beginning of the universe without mentioning the concept of God." And astrophysicist Fred Hoyle said, "I have always thought it curious that, while scientists claim to eschew religion, it actually dominates their thoughts more than it does the clergy."

## The Problem of Pain

We have a problem with suffering only if there is a God. If there isn't, pain is simply there, without reason, meaning, purpose. Yet something ineradicable in us craves all three. If we do have those specifically human hungers, which no other entity we know of suffers, why are we the only species thus cursed with hungers for food that doesn't exist? Some of us would say that if there is no God and we have to deceive ourselves until death with the illusion that we have some purpose, then why not go all the way and deceive ourselves that we do, in fact, have ultimate meaning? The atheists' excuses for going on—like Nietzsche's conviction that we are (momentarily) supermen, or Marx's conviction that we contribute manure to a workers' paradise we will never enjoy, or Camus's conviction that we can assuage our ultimate absurdity with bitchery—are much less satisfying.

Pascal put it best. At death, there is an iron dichotomy: Either we go on (in some way), or we don't. No other alternative. One option (we go on) is appealing; the other (we stop) is appalling. Since I have no way whatever to find out which it is, I might as well choose the appealing option and live a life that says not only will I go on but also all this anguish is ultimately redemptive. If I'm wrong, I'll never find out I was! Carl Sagan isn't going to be on the other side of the door of death, thumbing his nose and saying, "I told you so, idiot!" He's gone too.

Physical evil could have a purpose, at least for those who have achieved the use of reason. Suffering is essential to discover our good fortune in having been born at all. Who could appreciate light without having suffered the lonely darkness? Who could value warmth who has never been cold? Who could appreciate health who has never undergone terrifying illness? Without death to show us the transitory preciousness of everything, we would live like spoiled children. That is why so many who live as if death were an illusion never value anything, even life itself.

We hardly pause to realize it, but every minute of our lives is suffering, at least in the broadest sense of giving up something we are comfortable with in the hope of getting something better. Leaving the warm womb of the blankets is suffering—just as leaving the original womb was—but if we avoid leaving, we avoid life. Weaning, potty training, schooling, making it through adolescence, working, marrying, having children, growing old—all are suffering, in the hope of something more life-giving.

Even unmerited suffering, as Viktor Frankl showed, can be an opportunity. The key is in one's attitude. We have all known people in unspeakable pain and fear who react with whining or with anger or with denial. And we have also known people who face suffering with dignity. This is one reason Christians believe they have a unique take on God: Their God faced despair with dignity and came out the other side reborn.

None of that, of course, faces Ivan Karamazov's anguish. What about the suffering of the innocent, of those as yet incapable of seeing suffering as an invitation to more profound living? One response a high school senior gave is a clue to an answer, though not an answer: "If you can comprehend, then you can grow; if not, then it's no more than the sad suffering of a dumb beast." Job's greatest torment wasn't his physical pain; it was his sense of the unfairness of it, of the betrayal of the love he had given God for a lifetime. A child's suffering is lamentable but nowhere near as eviscerating as that of someone trying to believe. In the end, the theist clings to the belief that God has an infinitely broader perspective, that—in truth—each life, however brief and painful, is a brief patch of gray on an infinite light. The only other alternative is a pitiful patch of light on an infinite darkness.

Theists believe that God tolerates evil to preserve human freedom. God set a limit on his omnipotence in order to give humans intelligence and the freedom to use it well or badly. God could indeed have done what B. F. Skinner tried to do: bring us beyond freedom and dignity, where we would fulfill God's will for us exactly as every other species does. But apparently this experiment in freedom meant more to God than the slavish conformity of all other beings. Apparently God wanted to invent love, freely given, and along with it human dignity—so clearly embodied by Jesus in his passion. You don't want people to love you slavishly because you've infected them with some kind of love potion. The obsequiousness of robots is not enough.

## Occam's Razor

If there is a God, the question of his logical superfluity is moot, just as the pointlessness of an appendix doesn't negate its existence. Science can explain many phenomena—both physical and mental—that we previously suspected were the province of witch doctors. The extreme physicalist insists that all mental processes arise in the body, yet the opposite is also true, as in psychosomatic illness (and, apparently, healing). When I blush, it's my conscious realization of having goofed that triggers a physical reaction, not the other way around. Mind can control matter—or at least not be overwhelmed by it.

Dawkins's chimp seems at first blush to give credence to the possibility that consciousness arose by mere chance. But we tend to overlook that the chimp had the exercise set up for him, and we can only guess that somebody had to keep the restless chimp in his chair and focused on the computer. Sagan used similar slick arguments when he said in *Cosmos,* "One day, quite by accident, a molecule discovered a way to make crude copies of itself." I was so astonished that I wrote in the margin, "That was one [expletive deleted] clever molecule!" How could a brainless molecule discover anything? Sagan made the same claim for the evolution of the eye. One day "quite by accident" a trilobite found ways to store light crystals in his eye sockets, and thus the world could see! How fortunate the poor thing had eye sockets all ready and waiting, but how did that trilobite know there was light to be found if it had no eyes? I have a couple of mildly advanced degrees, but I have no idea what light crystals are, much less where to look for them. When I'm at the chalkboard in the classroom, I'd enjoy having an eye in the back of my head to watch what the enemy is doing, but no mental wrenching can bring me to the explosive discovery that the witless trilobite pulled off so facilely.

Science may be able to prove that chemicals and electricity spontaneously generated human self-awareness, but I defy it to explain evident realities that scientism would scorn, all those specifically human activities simpler folk associated with the soul: honor, selfless love, wisdom, virtue, humor, the need for reason, meaning, purpose. None of those activities is reducible merely to the body or the brain—both of which we share with other animals. Monogamous marriage is not rational; neither is having children. But neither of them is irrational; they are *beyond* rational. To say that strict logic is the only way to truth is reductionism in the highest degree. Truth is greater than facts.

My dictionary takes forty-three very tightly printed lines to define *love*. When I come to the end, I say to myself, "Is that all love is? I wish I knew as little about it as that Noah Webster did." On the other hand, a muddy little boy in a doorway with a fistful of droopy dandelions or a little girl with meticulously cornrowed hair says "love" too—in a far richer, more captivating, closer-to-the-real-truth way. Not as certain as a definition, but far more satisfying.

In the aptly titled "The Invincible Ignorance of Science," physicist Brian Pippard wrote:

> The phenomenon of consciousness—i.e., private self-awareness—is intrinsically beyond the range of the scientific method. You can't share my self-awareness, as I cannot share yours. . . . What is surely impossible is that a theoretical physicist, given unlimited computing power, should deduce from the laws of physics that a certain complex structure is aware of its own existence.

No strictly scientific objection to God has the slightest value, because God would transcend the competence of purely objective, rational analysis. One cannot deal with God with only the cookie-cutter definitions of the left brain lobe. One also needs the more elusive—but more evocative—symbols of the right brain lobe that "feel out" a reality that defies capture. Science, unaided, can't accommodate God, just as it can't accommodate love or humor.

### The Emptiness of God

The public/private impasse seems, again, to deny the validity of anything other than left-brain assertions based on solely left-brain cognition. This viewpoint tries to deny the incontestable reality of human experiences available to ordinary people on the street. When I have a headache, that is an unshareable experience, yet it is nonetheless real. Can a woman explain in any remotely satisfactory way why she's stayed with the same man, despite his evident flaws, for forty years? Is there some strictly rational basis that would motivate anyone to be honorable when he or she could make a grand, illicit coup without detection? Are human beings no more than the rational animals in the left-brain philosophers' definition—no more than apes with implanted computers? Is that all Shakespeare and Bach and Helen Keller were?

"There are more things in heaven and earth, Horatio, than are dreamt of in your philosophy"—or in your science or even in your religion, for that matter. To encounter the whole truth, we would have to find someone whose outward-looking skills were equally balanced by his or her inward-looking skills—the skills of mystics and musicians and lovers, the knowledge that eludes language and logic. Someone like Teilhard de Chardin.

As for the putative Creator's dawdling approach to the ultimate arrival of humans, it could be that the Creator was/is impervious to time and pressure and thus not anthropomorphically anxious to get the job done. As for his inefficiency, it could be that efficiency was not as high on the Creator's priority list as it obviously was on Carl Sagan's.

### Negative Consequences of Belief

Admittedly, horrific inhumanities have been justified by appeal to religion, but it is rankly unfair to root the inhumanity in the religion rather than in the unscrupulous ways expedient people manipulated the minds of simpler folk who trusted both the religion and the leaders. As Bertrand Russell said, "Many men would rather die than think. Most of them do." Arguing that Christianity caused the Inquisition is as unjust as arguing that science caused Dr. Frankenstein.

"By their fruits you shall know them." True. But it is reprehensible to limit the fruits to jihad and the Crusades and the rape of the Americas, especially when they went directly counter to what an objective viewer knows to be the religion's basic claims. Moreover, it deftly omits Mohammed's creation of the first managed attempt to organize social justice, taxing every believer a proportion of his assets (not his income) yearly for the poor. It ignores the education, medical assistance, research, and outreach to the disenfranchised that Christianity has motivated for twenty centuries. As Pippard wrote:

> When we have chased out the mountebanks there remain the saints and others of transparent integrity whose confident belief is not to be dismissed simply because it is inconvenient and unshared. We may lack their gift of belief ourselves, just as we may be tone-deaf; but it is becoming in us to envy those whose lives are radiant with a truth which is no less true for being incommunicable.

### LEAPING THE ABYSS

Faith is not a blind leap in the dark. It is a calculated risk. But when all the calculation is done, there is still the risk; there is still a leap—whether it be the commitment of marriage or the commitment to an unseen God.

One January Sunday in that anguished year before ordination, I left the spiritual father's room after yet another go-around. He had said—again—that if I felt like a bucket of scum, I shouldn't take such a life-changing step as asking for ordination. "Yes, you're right . . . but . . . well . . ." It was noon, and all the other seminarians were going to lunch and then out skating. I couldn't stand being with those "normal" people, so I went to my room, closed the door, and paced, fussed, fretted. Finally I said, "I can't stand this anymore! I'll lie down. I'll go to sleep. I'll get away from it for a while."

I lay down, but I didn't fall asleep. Suddenly, I felt overwhelmed. I can only inadequately describe it as like drowning in light. I was unaware of the time or the room. But I was certain beyond doubt or proof that I was in the presence of God. I was filled with a sense—diametrically opposed to all I'd felt about myself for so long—that I was accepted. Later, I came back to my time and place. I knew only that I had left the spiritual father's room at about noon and I became aware of myself again at about two. I sat up, and I said—for the first time in thirty-two years!—"I'm a good man! And I'll be a good priest because I'm a good man!"

I grabbed my skates and went down to the skating lake. Everyone was back inside by then. And I skated around in big circles, and I shouted it out: "I'm a good man! And I never have to prove it to anyone else again!" If God accepted me, who was I to deny acceptance? I had what Descartes demanded: "evidence so clear and distinct I have no occasion to doubt it."

From that moment, all the Latin gibberish about the Trinity—or about anything else—became meaningless, unnecessary, as disposable as the first stage of a rocket. I had been ravished across the abyss. After that experience, atheism no longer had a chance.

# 3

# A SUSPICION OF TRANSCENDENCE

The world is charged with the grandeur of God.
  It will flame out, like shining from shook foil;
  It gathers to a greatness, like the ooze of oil
Crushed. Why do men then now not reck his rod?
Generations have trod, have trod, have trod;
  And all is seared with trade; bleared, smeared
    with toil;
  And wears man's smudge and shares man's smell:
    the soil
Is bare now, nor can foot feel, being shod.

—GERARD MANLEY HOPKINS, "GOD'S GRANDEUR"

The chapter title suggests both uses of the word _suspicion_. On the one hand, the strictly rationalist mind finds any suggestion of a nonphysical dimension to reality—much less actual immaterial realities themselves—highly suspicious. On the other hand, many less-single-minded folk suspect that there is in truth more out there than meets the everyday eye; they say, "There's got to be more than this." It's called a sense of the numinous.

The most readily accessible path to God is not the way of the Vedas or the Bible or the Koran, the way of the theologians or the greatest preachers or even the towering mystics with whom all religions have been blessed. The most sensible way is the way of the simple and untutored, the way of the primitive and the child, the way of wonder, curiosity, vulnerability, candor: an openness to the awesome.

The theologians and the preachers bypass it, since most of them generally presume it or—at least in the case of many theologians—consider it peripheral to the Subject they have been trained to profess. They pass over this simple approach to God even though the very root of the religion they profess is a felt connection to the transcendent. They keep trying to help people know about God, when most people simply want to know God.

## THE INDESCRIBABLE . . . ALMOST

The Roman poet Ovid captured that eerie feeling: *Numen est,* "This place is haunted." Not necessarily haunted with frightening spirits but rather with a presence beyond the ordinary. Primitives, less disenchanted and sophisticated than we, were far more familiar with such a numinous aura to their lives. For Native Americans, religion was all about relationships—among themselves and with their whole environment. Religion was connections. The very word *ecology* comes from the Greek *oikos,* which means "to be at home." Like any myth system, Native American religion gave a whole matrix of meaning to the days and weeks and years of life, a sense of sacredness in what busier people like Mr. Gradgrind call reality. It is a presence that many, many others who have shared lifeboat earth with us called the *anima mundi,* "the soul of the earth." When the government wrote to Chief Seattle in 1852 with an offer to buy his tribe's land, he wrote back:

> The earth does not belong to man, man belongs to the earth. All things are connected like the blood that unites us all. We did not weave the web of life, we are merely a strand in it. Whatever we do to the web, we do to ourselves. . . . Your destiny is a mystery

to us. What will happen when the buffalo are all slaughtered? The wild horses tamed? What will happen when the secret corners of the forest are heavy with the scent of many people and the view of the ripe hills is blotted by talking wires? . . . The end of living and the beginning of survival.

Chief Seattle was a prophet.

Again, we are not speaking of the rarefied encounters of the great mystics with the ravishing presence of the Otherworldly. We need only look at the sense of the eternal-in-the-present experienced and testified to by ordinary folk, like my experience detailed in the last chapter. The poet James Russell Lowell wrote of such a moment:

I remember the night, and almost the very spot on the hilltop, where my soul opened out, as it were, into the Infinite, and there was a rushing together of the two worlds, the inner and the outer. I could not any more have doubted that He was there than that I was. Indeed, I felt myself to be, if possible, the less real of the two.

Sometimes we sense it more simply: listening to the rhythm of the rain or the harrumph of the waves, seeing a deer silvered in a shaft of moonlight, holding a newborn infant, escaping from an accident, hearing the cry "It's over!" or "I love you too," learning that "she's going to pull through." One time I was sharing Christmas with a couple and their children and grandchildren who have become my family, my "at home." In a quiet time in the afternoon, I was sitting in front of the fireplace in one of the out-of-the-way rooms, a blanket around my shoulders, reading. And Courtney, a three-year-old little girl, came to the couch, crawled inside the blanket with her head against my chest, and fell asleep. The simple, sweet, warm trust. For a sixty-seven-year-old celibate, it was a heart-stopping time. That moment wasn't an experience of God, but it was a moment of wonderment, a lowering of my everyday defenses and concerns. I was ambushed by the really real, the truly important.

Vulnerability is the absolute prerequisite. You can't force such peak moments to happen; you can only be habitually open to them, unafraid to be caught off guard. This vulnerability is very difficult in the jungles of our cities, where everyone is on guard even in a public park. That might be a reason so many—especially our young, who used to be carefree—need to trigger chemical highs. They've never been taught how to achieve the real thing.

Unlike a temporary chemical high, you don't feel let down after an encounter with the numinous. The difference between a unitive experience and a drug high is that a connection to the numinous gives way to serenity that lasts. It revivifies your hope in what life can deliver. Unlike the victim of D.T.'s who imagines his room carpeted with rats, otherwise levelheaded and fair-minded people give evidence that numinous experiences are rooted in a reality not circumscribed and made anathema by the prejudices of rationalism.

Experiences of the numinous are moments of ecstasy—ekstasis, "to stand outside" the commonplace world. Like Alice beyond the looking glass, they are times when we sense the vibrant aliveness within the dullness of our routine days. It is a sudden shift in perspective, a connection where the ordinary becomes extraordinary. In one sense we are submerged and subdued by our own insignificance (awe), yet in another sense we feel equally overwhelmed by being included in this greatness (wonder). Eastern religions believe that such moments are a taste of nirvana. Western religions feel an intuition that subsumes time and space into a fifth dimension. We are suspended in an eternal present, aware that there is far more to life than we've settled for.

Psychologist William James described such insight: "It is as if there were in the human consciousness a sense of a reality, a feeling of objective presence, a perception of what we may call 'something there,' more deep and more general than any of the [five] special and particular senses." This experience is not an effect caused by an arbitrary act of the will. On the contrary, the moment seizes and controls the human subject, who is its victim rather than its cause. There is a difference between the sacredness we impose on objects (amulets, totems) and the sacredness we respond to (babies, sunsets). Awe is not simply an emotion. It is an intuitional insight into the largeness and richness of our context.

## TWO WAYS OF KNOWING

Two quite distinct—but equally valid—powers of the human mind are often associated (perhaps too facilely) with the left and right lobes of the brain. The left brain is analytic (taking things apart); the right brain is synthetic (putting things together). The left brain is strictly objective and, in the Jungian sense, masculine (in both males and females). It is associated with all the qualities too long stereotyped to the male: logic, decisiveness, cold calculation. The right brain is subjective and feminine (in both males and females). It is associated with all the qualities too long stereotyped to the female: empathy, inclusiveness, seeing things in context rather than in isolation.

In any act of faith, religious or secular, the left brain does all the calculation and then turns over the still inconclusive results to the right brain to see if it "feels right." Conversely, every scientific discovery begins in the right brain, with a hunch that the formulas we've contented ourselves with for so long may be inadequate or that there might be some hitherto undiscovered properties in bread mold or silicon chips. Then it turns that hunch over to the calculating left brain to prove it right or wrong. It is an essential, symbiotic relationship. The left brain results in knowledge; the right brain opens to understanding—and perhaps even wisdom. To probe ideas exclusively with the left brain to the exclusion of the right is heartless, soulless. To seek truth only with the right brain to the exclusion of the left usually is sentimental or blindly prejudiced and often chaotic. To reason in such a hamstrung way is to reason half-wittedly.

Nonetheless, left-brain rationalism is quite definitely in the saddle today. Our Gradgrind educational system deals almost exclusively with facts. Even poems are used not to move the human soul but to serve as quiz fodder. If there is a school budget crunch, the first victims are music and art because the SATs, measuring left-brain analytical skills, determine what's truly important. In business, the final arbiter is the bottom line. If one element of the operation is irretrievably unsalvageable, cut it off—and be damned the consequences to the human beings it affects. In battle, the ultimate criterion is winning, no matter what the cost in personnel and no matter whether the war itself is even objectively justifiable. In science, it is understandable that all subjective factors should be left at the lab door: "If my thesis is wrong, they'll take away my grant. I've invested too much of my life in this work to allow this new contrary data to slow me down." However, the lab—like the classroom, the boardroom, and the war room—is only a segment of a much larger picture: human life. Not everything that can be done should be done.

It is the right brain (often suppressed as too "mushy") that offers the human corrective. It sees that curious and eager children are more important than the syllabus; that workers are more than cogs in a machine; that customers are more than consumers to be milked; that soldiers are sons and daughters and not merely willing pawns; that bombed cities are filled with innocent civilians, each of whom is objectively more important than any objective or cause or ideology; that a fetus is the product of two human cells that, left alone, will not become a banana or a zebra—no matter how tragically inconvenient it is.

Nor is imagination at odds with knowledge. It is indeed a way of illuminating facts, even if its insights are more ambiguous and open ended than the strict formulas and definitions so sacred to scientism. When asked what a dance meant, the choreographer Martha Graham said, "Mean? Darlings, if I could *tell* you, I wouldn't have *danced* it!" If you want to understand Handel's *Messiah,* I don't hand you a score. If you want to know why fans love baseball, it will be of little help to study the physics and geometry of the game. In all those cases—and in the case of the sacred—you have to experience them. And you have to develop a sensitivity to the numinous, evolve the potential within you, in order to apprehend the holy.

If anyone knows any Catholic school or church that starts with evolving a felt connection to the transcendent *before* it moves to ritual and theology, I'd be happy to hear about it.

Wonder, curiosity, and openness are qualities found in nearly all children—unless they have been ground out of kids by inhuman living conditions, by Gradgrind schooling, by the put-your-mind-in-neutral media. But we also find wonder and openness in the greatest scientists: Einstein, Heisenberg, Madame Curie, Gödel. Those qualities are, in fact, the essence of scientific discovery. Psychiatrist Carl Jung wrote, "The main content of my work is not concerned with the treatment of neuroses but rather with the approach to the numinous. But the fact is that approach to the numinous is the real therapy, and inasmuch as you attain the numinous experiences, you are released from the curse of pathology." Rationalists try to subdue the infinite sea; poets merely enjoy its immensity.

The true scientist feels the same insatiable curiosity that infants and toddlers have. Writing in tribute on Max Planck's sixtieth birthday, Einstein wrote of the scientist's true motive:

"The emotional state that enables such achievements is similar
to that of the religious person or the person in love. The daily
pursuit does not originate from a design or a program but from
direct need." And elsewhere, "I came close to the conclusion
that the gift of fantasy has meant more to me than my talent for
absorbing positive knowledge." It is a sense of "something behind
objects that lay deeply hidden." Physicist Richard Feynman
said, "To solve any problem that has never been solved before,
you have to leave the door to the unknown ajar. You have
to permit the possibility that you do not have it exactly right."

If theologians had that same tolerance for ambiguity, the
Orthodox and Catholics would still be united, Galileo might
have been canonized, and Lutherans and Calvinists and Catholics
would all sit down to a table fellowship at which all agreed
that Christ was somehow more really present than anywhere
else. The lion might lie with the lamb without surrendering
his leonine ferocity.

Science, especially in this century, shares the same wonder,
the unexpectedness, the new potential, the "freshness deep down
things" that the poet senses. Matter is never dead; it is aswarm
with life. Magnify a stone or a piece of metal, and we find a
universe whirling with atoms. We yield to wonder, realizing that
the starlight we see tonight began its journey toward earth before
there were humans. There is so much precarious magic just
in being alive. We have a suspicion that there is so much more
"out there and in here" than we ever surmised. There is a true
kinship between the mystic and today's scientist; each has to
grasp the universe dynamically as it moves, vibrates, and dances.
Relativity claims that we must become part of the dance in
order to understand it. Buddhists conceive of an object as an
event, not a thing; therefore one has to be a participant rather
than merely an aloof observer. And we begin to suspect that
*God* is not a noun but a verb, that activity is the very essence
of all being. All matter—from the carouse of the universe

to the unpredictable whirring of subatomic particles—is fundamentally restless, never quiescent. As Augustine said, "Our
hearts are restless till they rest in Thee."

Ultimately, this suspicion of transcendence can lead to
what Rudolf Otto called the *mysterium tremendum,* "the overwhelming mystery," who/which is the endmost source of energy.
It is awe before something objective, truly there, outside myself
that causes an involuntary feeling of smallness. Augustine felt
the same fusion of humility and exaltation: "What is that which
gleams through me and smites my heart without wounding it?
I am both ashudder and aglow. Ashudder insofar as I am unlike
it, aglow insofar as I *am* like it."

This trembling is not fear but awe. A dog can cringe in
fear. Unlike fear, awe serves no biological function, for example,
to warn of danger. Awe is not being humiliated by a bully but
rather being humbled by unexpected love. This is not the warm,
fuzzy Jesus so often preached about in Christian churches. This
is the Presence that the writer of Hebrews warned of: "It is a
terrifying thing to fall into the hands of the living God!" (10:31,
TEV). This is *islam,* "surrender."

When we speak of the supernatural, then, we are speaking
not of something above and inaccessible but of something here
and now and supercharged with the grandeur of God. As
William Blake wrote, "Heaven in a grain of sand and eternity
in a flower."

But most of us are too desensitized, too spoiled with
luxuries we take for granted, too busy with many things even
to sense the aliveness we crave and don't know where to find.

Picture Wordsworth in Times Square. "And all is seared
with trade; bleared, smeared with toil; / And wears man's smudge
and shares man's smell: the soil / Is bare now, nor can foot feel,
being shod." Human sensitivity has become armor-plated far
more than it was even in Hopkins's time. We live in jungle cities
of sirens and boom boxes, old tires, appliances, furniture, garbage,

rusty cars, abandoned houses, weeds, graffiti. All around us
pulse the rage, the soullessness, the exploitation, the surly self-
absorption. We put up defensive force fields—the invisible
blinders, the Walkman, the cell phone—numbing us to intrusions, giving us the illusion we are still somehow connected.

We settle for a "realistic" acceptance of what seems incon-
trovertibly the way things are. "Nobody can change anything."
We confuse vulnerability with weakness, defenselessness.
We adjust to the humdrum and practical, which then become
the norm, the stunting we share with everybody else. Therefore
we don't notice how impoverished we are—though we feel
the hungry emptiness somewhere in the depths of what might
have been.

Somehow, that Teflon desensitizing coalesced for me
in an experience I had thirty years ago, the only time I was ever
in the Louvre museum. In a hall crammed with what seemed
semiclassical junk, I suddenly came upon the Venus de Milo.
I was mesmerized. The sheen on the marble looked as if, were
I allowed to touch it, the skin would pulse with life. I collapsed
onto a bench and stared. My numinous daze was broken by a
portly, heavily cologned, unarguably American woman followed
by her husband in his madras shorts, beslung with cameras,
a dead cigar butt clamped in his jaw. As he passed, like an ox
rounding a grindstone, he muttered, "All right, we've seen the
goddamn Venus de Milo. Where's the goddamn Mona Lisa?"

Not much chance he'll have an encounter with the
*mysterium tremendum* anytime soon.

On the other hand, as someone once said, "If there is
Bach, there must be God."

# 4

## NEBULAE AND NEUTRINOS, QUASARS AND QUARKS

Were you there when I made the world?
    If you know so much, tell me about it.
Who decided how large it would be?
    Who stretched the measuring line over it?
    Do you know all the answers?
What holds up the pillars that support the earth?
    Who laid the cornerstone of the world?
In the dawn of that day the stars sang together,
    and the heavenly beings shouted for joy.

                        —JOB 38:4–7, TEV

Someone said of the physicist Max Planck that he forgot his faith when he went into his lab, and forgot his science when he went into church. In my benighted years studying theology, when the professors were blithely demythologizing Scripture, I was caught in the same kind of schizophrenic doublethink. (In fact, the only thing that kept me going was knowing that the Scripture profs still offered Mass each morning.)

The year after my ordination, I was due to give a homily on the Feast of the Ascension, so I got myself into a sort of semi-lotus position and tried to get into the scene. I walked with Jesus and the other disciples out to Bethany. I could smell their sweat and feel the chalky dust between my toes in my sandals. Jesus raised his hand, blessed us, then began to rise into the heavens. Then what? I got Jesus suspended in midair, as in paintings of the Ascension, but. . . . So my imagination let him keep going, like a missile in low gear. This provoked a few unsettling questions. Did he go through the Van Allen belt? Was he radioactive? Did he keep going through the endless cold of space, onward and upward, until he finally came to the thin, thin membrane that separates the physical universe from heaven, then slip through it—*boop!*—like an insertion through a self-sealing tire?

You can see how literal my understanding of Scripture still was, even after all those courses. It raised even further questions. If heaven and hell are, by definition, outside time and space where nothing physical exists, where do they get the oysters for those pearls in the pearly gates, the gold to pave the heavenly streets, the gut to string all those harps, and all the coal to keep the hellfires burning from the rise of *Homo sapiens* until now? Where do you locate a body (even a resurrected one) in a dimension of reality where bodies have no meaning or purpose? If Jesus went "up" from Bethany into the heavens above, an old lady in Australia on her final journey would go "up" in precisely the opposite direction. And never the twain shall meet.

Until then, I had complacently impounded all I knew about religion in the right lobe of my brain with all the symbols, and all I knew about science and cosmology in the left lobe with all the definitions and formulas. And never the twain could meet—jostling and confounding one another (to say nothing of me). But to keep an honest mind, I had, once again, to invite the lion and the lamb to lie down together, without the lion devouring the lamb or the lamb emasculating the lion.

In light of the legitimate claims of each source of understanding, I had to go back and rework, not the realities, but the inadequate metaphors I'd been using to help me understand them. When we explore invisible entities (like electrons and the elect in heaven), we resort to physical symbols for beings that are not themselves palpable. We use hearts, for instance, to symbolize love, because when one is in love, the heart flutters faster in the presence of the beloved. But even the hearts on valentines are idealized; imagine if you sent your one-and-only a picture of a literal heart! God the Father appears as an old man with a beard when we know that God is incapable of aging (and is, in fact, younger than we), that God has no genitals and is therefore of neither physical sex. Surely, if the angel Gabriel had had to depend on a set of wings (no matter how huge) to bring God's request from "way up there" to Mary in Nazareth, he would have had to start his flight somewhere around the time of the big bang, and when he got there, he would have been panting pretty painfully.

This doesn't mean that heaven, hell, God, and his messages don't exist. It means only that they don't exist in any physical way. Alas, physical metaphors are the only way we space-time folk can really begin to understand objects. Green is *like* chewing mint leaves; my experience of God before ordination was *like* drowning in light; the fulfillment of the kingdom is *like* a party; Jesus' ascension was *like* going through a black hole into a kind of parallel universe. But none of these "likes" are "it." Comfortingly, as we shall see, in the last century, science has had to go back and do the same kind of metaphor retooling with Newton's physics.

We can live more or less assured lives because there is always a reliable pattern to them. Night and day keep yielding to one another; the seasons roll around more or less predictably; infancy opens into childhood, then adolescence, adulthood, old age, and death. Without giving mind to it, we rely on the dependability of cause and effect: Drop a brick out the window, it will go down; drink too much, you risk liver problems; use a credit card, sooner or later you'll pay. Though I never met them, I'm absolutely certain that you had two parents, one male, one female. Even in a case of amnesia, we can be sure that the victim did have some kind of real past. In science, if an experiment gives results one way today, it ought to give the same result next week. Dependence on cause and effect is the foundation of the scientific method, criminal detection, investigative reporting, proof for the existence of God, and just plain day-to-day life. Even when we deal with calculated risks—as in the stock market, at the racetrack, at the altar, or in the church—we like to cut the unpredictable down to a minimum.

But when things get out of hand, we become uneasy, sometimes even desperate, when we can't nail down the cause(s) of an unexpected effect. A seemingly happy teenager commits suicide. Students go berserk and shoot up their school. The *Challenger* space shuttle blows up. No one says, "Oh, well, it was an accident." We want answers. Unless we can isolate the causes, we'll make the same mistakes next time. Something had to cause that explosion: O-rings, cold weather, a combination of the two? The human purpose is to know and try to understand. We get frustrated when that urge is stymied.

The universe that Isaac Newton described for us is a model of dependable, clockwork, cause-and-effect predictability. Every object in the universe turns on its axis and revolves around something else, and that set turns around something else. Each planet has a definite position, direction, and speed. We know where Mars is today and can calculate a course for a rocket to impact it on a particular date months or even years down the line. The physics are as clean and clear as an expert calculating a billiard shot or the trajectory of a bowling ball. We thought the same reassuring pattern occurred even in the tiniest components of the universe. We had proof of it, right there in our physics books: a picture of an infinitesimally tiny replication of a solar system, with the nucleus as its sun and its planet electrons whizzing peacefully around it.

But then, in the late 1920s, behind our backs, Albert Einstein and Werner Heisenberg (and a host of others) shook the whole thing out of whack. In effect, they dematerialized matter. Even many youngsters today who have taken good physics courses don't seem to realize that. But the two greatest scientific discoveries of the century—relativity and quantum theory—threw certitude out the cosmic window. Therefore, if you're looking for scientific proof of anything, you can no longer expect, as Descartes did, "evidence so clear and distinct I have no occasion to doubt it." Not even in physics, the hardest of the hard sciences. It's not called the atomic *dogma*. It's called the atomic *theory*. Genuine scientists are far more humble and hesitant than most people naively believe them to be.

## RELATIVITY

In the theory of relativity, Einstein showed that the position of the observer skews the evidence. "Up," for instance, as with the Ascension, has meaning only relative to where you happen to be at the time. A woman reading a book on a train would be, from her viewpoint, sitting at rest, but to a farmer watching the train, she'd be moving pretty fast. If you could hitch a ride on an object moving at the speed of light, you would be at rest on it; time in your biological clock would tick away just as it had back on earth. But if you could turn around and come back, most of your friends would be dead. Because of your speed, you would have been traveling (relative to you) about a year or so, but they would have lived forty or fifty years (relative to them).

More important, there is the formula all of us have heard but few have pondered: $e = mc^2$. That means energy (e) equals mass (m) times the speed of light (c) squared. Reversing that, it follows as the night does the day that mass times the speed of light squared *is* energy. In other words, the ordinary bulky objects we see and heft are not really solid at all but are fundamentally locations of energy. Thus, if you could crack open the most basic component of what we call physical reality, what you would (probably) find is nonextended energy. The rock that took the skin off your shin is not really solid at all. It's a swarm of moving particles, and most of it is empty space. If you could compress all the rock's components together, it would be less than a millionth of the object you see. Conversely, if you could blow up a hydrogen atom to the dimensions of the Astrodome, the nucleus would be a tiny bit of grit on the floor, and the electron would be up at the roof, and the rest would be, well, empty.

Thus, massy objects we see are what Eastern mystics call *maya,* "illusion." But do we impose the form on the objects we see, or is it actually there? If not, how do we explain why, when each of us sees the complex of particles that make up a chair, we both know that it's a place to sit and not a place to get a drink of water? Despite the conundrums, Einstein's theories were validated by the atomic bomb—which is pretty impressive evidence.

## QUANTUM THEORY

It gets worse. There's also quantum mechanics. Werner Heisenberg's principle of uncertainty shows that the symbol for the atom we've all taken for granted as a trustworthy representation of submicroscopic particles is no more accurate than the hearts on valentines. For one thing, electrons jump orbits without apparent cause. For another, sometimes an electron acts like a pellet but at other times like a wave. If you could fire an electron from an electron "gun" at a wall with two holes in it, the electron would be as likely to go through both holes at once because at that instant it was a wave. Is an electron a pellet or a wave? Yes.

If you ran full tilt at a wall, you'd expect to be flattened against it and slide down on the same side. But a subatomic particle could hurtle toward the barrier and appear on the other side without leaving a hole behind it. If that weren't true, we'd have no digital watches, PCs, or transistor radios. No! Yes.

What's more, you can ask, "Where is the particle, and how is it moving?" But you can't answer both questions at the same time, since the evidence you need to discover one distorts the evidence about the other. In order to "see" an electron, you have to bounce a bundle of energy off it—and in the process, the electron's situation is changed. In James Trefil's handy analogy, if you want to find out if a car is coming through a long tunnel, the only way you can be sure is to send another car zooming from the other end, then wait for the crash. The impact will tell you that the car is there, but it's no longer the original car. You can locate the car (electron), but in doing so you change not only its momentum but also its direction.

Quantum physicists try to track down and explain the behavior of atoms and their members: nuclei, electrons, positrons, neutrinos, quarks—the whole nuclear family. But when you read even their popularized conclusions, it tends to cross your eyes exactly the way John Courtney Murray did when he was teaching us Bernard Lonergan's Latin Trinity text, in Latin. Electrons, you see, are not actually "there" in the same way your stove and the Sears Tower and the rings of Saturn are "there." (That is equally true of God, if God exists.) Rather than being a point or strictly a wave, an electron is rather a blur around the nucleus, more like a wave packet, a center of force, or—even less satisfyingly—a tendency to exist. During observations (in the tunnel), it seems a solid entity, but between observations it's, well, somewhere. Maybe.

When you're studying an electron (or God), how do you describe a not-quite-thing? Scientism claims that subatomic particles are actually "there" but are too minute and unpredictable to be observed, whereas God, by definition, cannot in any way be observed, no matter how incredibly powerful our instruments become. Thus, says scientism, God is irrelevant to rational discourse and dismissible. We could pose the question, though, whether such particles as electrons, neutrinos, and positrons are really "there," as we are, or are just approximate fictions, practicable metaphors, like angels for divine messages. Surely some superenergized, supercompacted force is present; atomic power proves that. But what is it, really? Well, uh, nobody's quite able to say.

An individual elementary particle doesn't really have a known or knowable history as we do: "I lived in Rochester from 1965 to 1987, and in the Bronx since then." Rather, it has a smudge of possible histories from which we can predict where it's going, though some are more likely than others, have a greater probability. In fact, chaos theory involves making a list of all possible outcomes and assigning to each the probability that such and such subatomic effect will happen in any single trial. But in the case of elementary particles, the consolingly sharp sense of cause is lost. And that loss of certitude disturbs many people, whether the question is about the trustworthiness of our senses or our religion's scriptures.

Yet, like symbols, probability is better than nothing at all. Most of our choices and beliefs are, in fact, calculated risks, some of which have higher trustworthiness than others. In the commonsense world, we can have a better chance of a successful marriage if we've known and trusted one another for a long time. Television networks can give remarkably reliable predictions of election results even when half the polls are still open. Insurance companies risk millions on actuarial statistics that predict what percentage of the population will reach certain ages. Las Vegas casino owners calculate the odds and make certain that the house always wins. It's important to remember that "not proven" and "not completely certain" are not the same as "false."

Seekers for God can learn from the practitioners of science, especially in curbing their expectations—and their demands for evidence. Both have to evolve a tolerance for ambiguity, paradox, and polarity—not either/or but both contraries at the same time. Complementarity.

## COMPLEMENTARITY

Wit and comedy can't be taught in any logical, rational way. You either have it, or you don't; you either get it, or you don't. When the stooge threatens Jack Benny with "Your money or your life," Benny's long pause gets a laugh because at least part of the audience sees the reason for it. A literalist would have a difficult time listening to Robin Williams for very long, and predicting what his next thought is going to be is like trying to anticipate which way a kernel of corn is going to pop. Yet his routines are a marvel of timing, factual knowledge, and an uncanny ability to instantly fuse together two seemingly radically incompatible ideas.

The same thing is true of experiencing classical music. It is an exhilarating mixture of tone, rhythm, and mathematical harmonics, but neither Mozart nor his captivated audience needs a slide rule or a timer to figure it out. One could say the same about a genuine appreciation for poetry. My senior honor English students can pick out instances of assonance or alliteration like magpies in a town dump, but few have any sense of the poet's purpose in using it in any particular place. They are in no way moved by it, nor do they have the slightest sensitivity to nuance or a shift in mood signaled by a change in word choice or sounds. Their Gradgrind education has honed their left-brain rational skills to surgical acuity, but their right brains are nearly dead.

The left and right brain lobes complement one another. They have skills as contrary as those of *Star Trek*'s Mr. Spock and *The Grapes of Wrath*'s Ma Joad, as different as trying to find the truth from an accused criminal by administering a lie-detector test or by facing him with his mother. (I'd go with the mother every time.) Yet each brain lobe supplies significant data that the other is incapable of accessing. Even though at first they seem contrary and incompatible, they offer a more nearly complete understanding together than either one can alone.

Probably the most familiar embodiment of that polarity of opposites is the Taoist picture of the yin and yang, a circle bisected by a wavy line separating a black hemisphere from a white one, each with a small circle of the other color embedded in it. It is a synthesis of rest and movement, contrast and concord, an eternal interplay of opposites: masculine and feminine, hot and cold, man and woman, suffering and serenity, sacred and secular. It is a dynamic interplay between polar forces, like the contrary poles of a magnet that—fused—create a force neither possesses alone. The lion lies down with the lamb without either absorbing the other's unique qualities.

The same principle helps explain (at least a bit better) the electron as wave and particle, humans as beasts and angels, creation as evolution and Genesis, Max Planck as physicist and believer. At first—and for those who give the contrary factors only cursory attention—the two elements seem as radically incompatible as fire and water. (But don't forget the Native American name for whiskey.) Actually, the two polar opposites act as a balance and corrective to each other, just as it is always prudent to have on any committee a fiery liberal and an ironfisted conservative to provide the group antidotes for each viewpoint. Rather than depending on the clear-cut dualism of Descartes, which drew a rigid line between the knower *(res cogitans)* and the world *(res extensa)*, we have to become involved in the problem and walk around inside its apparent conflicts in order to understand them fully. Not stone-faced judges but benign and impartial arbitrators. Complementarity is an organic, holistic attempt to harmonize contrary realities, both of which we know are "there."

## SCIENCE'S ACTS OF FAITH

In her remarkable book *The Fire in the Equations,* Kitty Ferguson outlined five commonsense truths we have to assume in order to "do" either science or religion. These are truths that are self-evident and incapable of rational proof, truths we simply have to accept on faith as true or we are intellectually immobilized:

1. The universe is rational. It has patterns, predictability, symmetry. Causes generate effects, and therefore it is not futile to study those relationships, as it would be to parse the ravings of a mad person.

2. The universe is accessible. It can be (at least partly) understood; objective facts can give rise to reliable subjective opinions.

3. The universe is contingent. It could have been different, and there are causal factors (if not purposeful reasons) why things are as they are and not otherwise.

4. The universe is objective. It is a reality that doesn't yield to our preferences.

5. The universe is a unity. It operates, everywhere, by unchanging laws.

If this were not so, not only would science be impossible, but it would be hopeless to figure out where you lost your keys.

I would make bold to add another truth: Order is not self-generating. Having directed about fifty musicals, with both kids and their parents, I know that there is not the remotest chance that forty people on a stage—no matter how talented, intelligent, willing, or unflagging—would come up with the dance-off in the gym of *West Side Story* without direction. Further, knowing what I know of those Siamese twins Talent and Ego, I'm just as convinced that professionals couldn't pull it off either. The alternative to someone/something in charge is chaos, and only chaos. And if that is true of humans who have brains (and training), it must be even truer of mindless celestial bodies and subatomic particles. How did they organize themselves into the great choreographed carouse of the heavens and the Dionysian hip-hop of the atom—all by themselves? With no brains?

As Thomas Edison said, "We don't know a millionth of one percent about anything."

## THE UNIVERSE AND EVOLUTION:
## CHANCE OR CHOICE?

Many scientists struggled against the evidence for the big bang theory of the origin of the universe because it seemed to argue for a beginning *ex nihilo* and therefore would require some independent cause, namely, God. Today, it seems nearly incontrovertible that the universe is expanding and that therefore there was a beginning—at least of this universe as we know it now. Therefore, we have only two alternatives: It happened by either chance or choice, accident or Creator. No one of honest mind could resent the rigid exclusion of religious convictions from the antiseptic inquiries of science. But the obverse should also be true: Atheism, the desire to avoid admitting to a God, cannot be allowed to skew the evidence either.

Did time and matter begin to exist at the big bang that caused this particular universe? Or was the "stuff" of it always there? Was the seed of our universe a singularity, an entity of zero volume and infinite density, smaller, as Carl Sagan said, "than a point in mathematics"? (This is about as close to nothing as you can get.) At some time in the future will the universe collapse again into that infinitesimal singularity—only to explode again and again and again? (This would make us humans far less significant even than we believe ourselves to be now.) Did our universe emerge like a bubble at the end of an umbilical cord off another universe? Was the big bang an *ex nihilation* or merely a transformation? We can't answer the questions from reason alone. To argue for the necessity of a First Cause (as Aquinas did) begs the question if, in fact, matter is without beginning or end rather than God's being without beginning or end. It must be one or the other.

But the result of that accident/creation is not in doubt. Unless our acts of faith in the objectivity of the cosmos and the dependability of our intelligence are delusional, we are witnesses to a near-infinite carouse of the heavens. This is the point: It is not a carouse in the sense of a rioting mob, but it is an incredibly well choreographed dance, from the Busby Berkeley immensity of the universe to the delicate pas de deux of the hydrogen atom. We don't invent the periodic table with its mesmerizing complexity and gradations, nor the laws of physics, which science assures us are the same everywhere in the universe. The evidence comes to us from "out there."

Sagan wrote, "It is only by the most extraordinary coincidence that the cosmic slot machine has this time come up with a universe consistent with us." And with no one to insert the quarter and pull the lever! *Extraordinary* is far too puny a word. How does one get order out of chaos by sheer chance? How does one get laws out of luck? If one believes that the obvious design of the cosmos occurred by sheer chance, one would also have to be open at least to the possibility that if one dropped an atomic bomb on Pikes Peak, it might come down a working Disneyland. Perhaps that might be in the realm of possibility, but it overloads my meager mental circuits. Not extraordinary; improbable. More likely, impossible.

If I chance upon a pumpkin belting out "Hey, Big Spender," I have to argue that there's a speaker inside, since no pumpkin has that capability. Reason argues that no effect can be greater than its causes. I may not be able to access all the causes, as in the case of a suicide or the *Challenger* explosion, but at least in the macro world of common sense, there must have been some confluence of agents that resulted in those events. Occam's razor argues that beings are not to be postulated unless they are inescapable. One is stuck with a choice between a nearly infinite succession of fortunate accidents or a completely infinite, purposeful Creator.

The same holds true for the evident evolutionary pro-
gression from inanimate to vegetative to animate to intelligent
beings. All the evidence seems to point to a developing complexity in life that *seems* purposeful, finally arriving at beings
who are self-aware. To argue that natural selection accounts for
those varieties better suited to survive is, at the very least, an
inaccurate use of words; only an intelligent entity can select or
choose or discover. Sagan wrote, "I find it elevating that our
universe permits the evolution of molecular machines as intricate and subtle as we are." Permits? If human beings are no
more than intricate and subtle machines, perhaps yes. But there
is a great deal about me that I can't root in a mechanism, even
something as marvelous as the human body and brain. How
does a machine account for honor, self-sacrifice, courage, loyalty,
wisdom, hope, magnanimity, altruism, the need for meaning?
To abridge human beings to only bodies and brains (much less
to bags of chemicals and electricity) is too reductionist by far.

Like the apparent design of the universe, the factors
needed to permit entities as intricate and subtle as we are—
those elements required to fall into place at precisely the right
times—appear to be astronomical to the nth power. The earth
is tilted at twenty-three degrees; if it were not, we would have
no seasons. If the crust of the earth were ten feet thicker, there
would be no oxygen. If the oceans were only a few feet deeper,
carbon dioxide and oxygen would have been absorbed, and
no vegetable life could exist. Gravity, the same force that pulls a
thrown ball down, also prevented the universe from expanding
so rapidly that life as we know it could never emerge. If the
expansion were one-billionth of a percent larger, life would have
been impossible. Lecomte de Nouy argued that even if a new
combination of molecules arose by random chance every millionth of a second, it would take longer than the earth's life
to form a chain leading to life. The odds are the number one

followed by ninety-six zeros. Yet life existed on earth less than a billion years after its formation.

Two factors in evolution stretch chance to the breaking point: time and coordination.

First, time. A single bacterium contains about two thousand enzymes, but according to Fred Hoyle, the odds of obtaining them all at a random trial are 1 in 1,040,000, and enzymes are only one step in the formation of life. Thus, the chance that life originated by random ordering of organic molecules is not meaningfully different from zero. In a famous analogy, Hoyle said that the likelihood was as close to possibility as a tornado whipping through an airplane junkyard and leaving behind a working 747, even given eight billion years.

Second, coordinating all the factors that had to come together at precisely the right time for an effect to occur staggers the imagination. Bat radar, for instance. In order for that skill to come about, the following had to occur *at the same time:* the special physical apparatus to make sounds, specialized ears to hear the echoes, brains to interpret the sounds, bodies and wings adapted to swoop for the insects detected.

Lotta luck there, Carl.

The human eye alone seems to demand a Designer; even Charles Darwin was hung up on that. Eyes are impossible for the most brilliant human to construct. We have two, so we can see in three dimensions. Each eye has a lens and bellows that work automatically, even for mentally impaired persons. Eyes take color pictures sixteen hours a day, and you never have to change the film or send it out to be developed. And very often, when they're damaged, they repair themselves! What's more, the brain behind those eyes turns the pictures into abstract ideas!

If you found a watch ticking away in the desert, or a Coke bottle on the moon, or a turtle perched on a fence post, could any sane person be convinced they got there by chance?

## CONTRAILS OF GOD IN THE UNIVERSE

We can tell much about an artist's personality, what he or she likes and dislikes, from his or her work. You can tell the differences between Rembrandt and Mondrian, Handel and Gershwin from the ways they handle the same basic materials. So too with the Architect of the Universe.

We know that the Mind Behind It All is into order: the predictable courses of the stars, the regularity of the seasons, the patterns in objects that allow us to use universal words like *oak, circle, chair.* But God also reveals a whimsicality that refuses to be boxed in; God is also into surprise. Every planet does follow predictable patterns, yet each one is unique: fiery, chalky, glacial, ringed with debris. Every snowflake in Antarctica is made on exactly the same pattern, yet no two are alike. Identical twins have exactly the same DNA, yet their fingerprints are unique. Even two sides of the same human face are not mirror images of one another. We find perfect geometrical shapes, in fact, only in man-made artifacts. The hexagons in beehives and the diamond shapes of sunflower seeds seem a bit lopsided; no one could call any tree trunk a true cylinder; even the earth is a rather bulgy sphere. We could make the case that though the Creator is into order, he is not a fanatic about it, like the people who want to bring the Leaning Tower of Pisa into plumb. We can only be grateful. Imagine a forest in which every tree was a perfect cylinder, every apple a perfect sphere, every lumberjack a Brad Pitt clone.

The Architect of the Universe also seems undeniably into evolution and growth, though again, he seems in no great hurry about it as we are, nor is he very efficient. He's willing instead to dawdle with fantastic species like dinosaurs and pterodactyls before moving on to more complex enterprises. It appears that the Creator made rocks to sit and await the uses of human ingenuity; plants to give oxygen, food, and beauty; animals to challenge humans, provide food and clothing and at times even companionship. He made humans to learn and to love—and, of all species, to continue to evolve their specific human nature until they die, as witness again the spectrum of humanity from Dr. Josef Mengele to Dr. Albert Schweitzer.

But one quality that religions attribute to the Deity is not very obvious from the nature he created: providence. If there is really a God, then his nature and personality are not the result of human projection. If it were, we could surely have come up with a more congenial one. Nature is savage and implacable, from the raging tornado to the shark to the conscienceless cat. If we are to establish that God cares for us, we can find that attribute only in the many ways and cultures to whom (they claim) he revealed himself Person-to-person.

Perhaps, since it treads on the toes of science, this might be a good place to say at least a word about miracles. Unless we count the true miracles that we take so much for granted, like the human eye, a baby's fingers, the message system of our DNA, miracles are quite rare. If they weren't, the concept would be vacuous. Many of the miracles in any religion's scriptures are quite likely symbolic—mediating truth, but not necessarily historical truth. But if miracles do in fact occur, they show that, as in so many things, the Creator is far more flexible than we would like him to be. As to the Christian belief in the virgin birth, one would think that the God who invented the ovum could quicken it any way he chose to. (The only Christian miracle that really counts, the Resurrection, will have to wait for later.)

We know from science that the solid marble hand of a statue is really a cloud of molecules continuously jostling one another in random directions. Their movements cancel one another out, so the hand remains inert. But if by chance (or God's intervention) all the molecules moved in the same direction at once, the hand would move. Not probable, but possible. Einstein said, "God does not play dice with the universe," to which Niels Bohr reputedly replied, "Albert, don't tell God what he can do." And Kitty Ferguson wrote:

In a universe which combines predictability and
freedom, insisting there was a violation of the fundamental laws of the universe if the waters parted for
the Israelites or even if Christ rose from the dead
might be tantamount to insisting that the Constitu-
tion of the United States is violated if traffic is
allowed to flow the wrong way on a one-way Fifth
Avenue for several hours to accommodate a
St. Patrick's Day parade.

Our experience of the Creator's power suggests that he is
totally "other" than we are, yet our experience of the numinous
suggests that he is also lurking beneath the surface of things.
It also suggests that this Being is both inexpressibly complex
and inexpressibly simple. Complementarity again. It is possible
that the universe reveals a God who is both its First Cause,
simpler than the most elementary particle, and its Final Cause,
the ultimately complex model and goal of it all, as Teilhard
de Chardin suggested.

In conclusion, Robert Jastrow, director of NASA's Goddard
Institute, wrote:

> For the scientist who has lived by his faith in reason,
> the story ends like a bad dream. He has scaled the
> mountains of ignorance; he is about to conquer the
> highest peak; as he pulls himself over the final rock,
> he is greeted by a band of theologians who have
> been sitting there for centuries.

# 5

## CROSSING THE ABYSS

Fill your minds with those things that are good
and that deserve praise: things that are true, noble,
right, pure, lovely, and honorable. . . . And the
God who gives us peace will be with you.

—PHILIPPIANS 4:8−9, TEV

At this point, at least some might agree that there is a
greater probability of a Creator than the alternative—that all
of what we know, including ourselves, came about merely from
a near-infinite series of most advantageous accidents. But so far,
we can tell very little about what he/she/it is—or at least is
remotely like. We have arrived only at the God of the Philosophers: the Uncaused First Cause, the Prime Mover, the Mind
Behind It All. At this point, we are like the first Everest climbers
at base camp, pretty sure that something is up there but without
too much basis upon which to say what it is.

For those brought up and indoctrinated in a religious
tradition, it is difficult to critically examine the incrustations
of belief assimilated as children. Their parents' admonitions and
precepts are embedded: Never talk to strangers; everybody on

welfare cheats (or it's the rich people who cause the need for welfare); roast beef is no good unless it's well-done (or raw). Such well-meaning folks continue to their deaths (which often are redundant) never even talking to "one of them," feuding over the same unexamined givens. This is too often true of the content of our religious beliefs, not only our religious practices, but also our ideas about God and therefore about the depth and richness of our connection to God.

Each Monday night I teach a Problem of God course at the university. There are a few full-time undergraduates, but most students have other jobs and are admirably slogging away to get that diploma. One week on a quiz regarding seventy pages in the text about God and suffering, I asked, "Give one argument against this statement: God does not exist." The results in nearly half the papers were unsettling: "Well, of course there's a God; how could all of this stuff have gotten here with-out God?" "God does exist; he sent his only-begotten Son to die for our sins." "God exists because the whole Bible gives testimony to him." None of them seemed to know the difference between an argument and an unsubstantiated assertion.

Few had given the slightest real thought to the possibility that God does not exist or to the possibility that their own understanding of God might be childishly cramped. The reasons for that are many. Primarily, their lives are chock-full of a great many "more important" and pressing problems (and all but one or two students are taking the course not to learn about God but to fulfill a university requirement). Also, in nearly every case, the last significant input in their understanding of God was ten years or so ago in high school, if they had it then. And even if they continue to worship regularly, the input they get from the pulpit is not (truth to tell) intriguing to the mind or stimu-lating to the heart or enlivening to the soul.

Yet all those students had previously heard me explain and discuss all we saw in the last three chapters of this book.

However, I had had only six weeks to challenge, in some cases, thirty years of unchallengeable notions. They had an ironbound (if totally unfocused and unreasoned) conviction not only that God exists but also that God is captured definitively in the God they learned of in grade school.

What I would like to do from this point on is to clear the decks. We will start from where we have struggled to get so far, the realization that there is some intelligent Entity at the root of all that exists, and push forward with completely open minds to understand what this God is like. We will examine God's nature and God's personality, unafraid either of questioning and refining our lifelong certitudes or of allowing the insights of other radically different viewpoints to enrich our own.

Even at this point, the God of the Philosophers is not totally unfocused. If the Artist's choices in using materials and honing their outcomes is a revelation of his personality, we know that this Instigator is into order and surprise and growth. If the Creator preceded time and space, we can also argue that he is timeless and immaterial. He is omnipotent; if there were some limit on him, he would not be the Supreme Being, merely an agent. It also follows that God is infinite, immutable, uncon-ditioned, and uncaused. Since God is perfect, it further follows that he had no need to create; there must have been some other reason for it. Perhaps God just likes stories, and since stories always hinge on the unpredictable, he wanted to create characters who would constantly surprise him. Further, since having life (without defining its form) is a greater perfection than being inert, he himself must be, at least in some sense, alive. Our experience of the numinous suggests that God is close by, immanent. Yet his pre-cosmos existence argues that he also must be wholly "other" than we are, transcendent. We cannot say that God lives or knows or wills or creates *as* humans do. If God created the cosmos from nothing, he didn't create as human artists or artisans (or parents) do, from previously existing materials; he created

more like (yet unlike) the way we produce ideas. God is not
remotely analogous to us; we are remotely analogous to God.
God is not anthropomorphic; humans are theomorphic.

The philosophers can lead us to the brink of a chasm.
On this side is what our unaided minds can discover about the
Deity from his works. Across the chasm—on the other side—
is what he is in himself. But only if God could reach across
that abyss and contact us could we discover that he is personal
(other than having intelligence and will) or that he is provident,
caring for us. Is this unapproachable Other also loving, merciful,
just? There is no way to find hints of those qualities in nature.
Therefore, the God of the Philosophers, the Uncaused First Cause,
is exempt from any atheist attacks that argue, "How could a
loving, merciful, just God allow thousands of children to suffer
and die?" The Deity started it all; live with that.

In our mellower or more religious moods, we can say,
"God clothes the lilies of the field, and his protective eye is on
the sparrow." But that same God created a world in which the
belly of Vesuvius could erupt in fire and kill thousands, and
the sparrow may distract his eye from the millions of human
beings throughout history who have died in wretchedness,
invoking his name in its many cultural forms. We cannot find a
moral or compassionate or provident God in the universe or in
nature (at least below the human). Nature is the dog-eat-dog
jungle; the predators prevail. Only the fittest, the toughest, the
uncaring are rewarded with survival. Nature and animals are
territorial, rapacious, self-absorbed. And that self-absorption is
replicated in unevolved humans, from the pugnaciousness in
industrial and military boardrooms to the indolence of study
halls in self-styled educational institutions: the beast in us, what
Freud called the id, the thing.

The God who called forth lion and lamb, hurricane and
heartfelt love, cancer and compassion could well be capricious,
even sadistic. There is undeniable evidence of it.

Still, there are hints of a softer side to the Creator even in nature, which is not unrelievedly ravening: solicitous motherhood in animals, protective fatherhood, even self-sacrifice (at least for one's own). It is difficult to stand in a field of spring wildflowers or to drive by a placid lake reflecting autumn leaves or to hold a newborn child and believe that God is all blood lust. Any image we have of God has to account for both suffering and serenity. Complementarity.

Traces suggesting a benevolence in the Creator are evident in at least some human beings. Our nature invites us to evolve beyond the predatory animal, the beast, the id, which is undeniably always within us. There is a spectrum in the human species ranging from Catherine the Great at one extreme (little better than a shark with access to a cerebral cortex) to Mother Teresa at the other (a little less than the angels). As we've noted, there are activities and qualities exclusive to the human species that cannot be reduced to the workings of either the body or the brain: honor, self-sacrifice, courage, loyalty, wisdom, hope, magnanimity, altruism, the need for meaning. If the Creator infused those potentials in us, it suggests something of what he values.

As far as we can tell, only the human species is pestered by the need to find a purpose for things and events; only human beings ask why. We are the only species we know of that can anticipate death—and yearn to survive it. We are the only ones given to discontent, who grumble, "There's got to be more than this." We are dissatisfied with the finite, the transitory, the incomplete. Only we are free *not* to fulfill the programming in our nature that invites us to evolve beyond mere beasts. No rock gets uppity and begins to grow; no carrot decides that the earth is richer on the other side of the fence and uproots itself; no sheep begins baaing the multiplication table. Conversely, no lion refuses to act leonine; no cabbage refuses food; no rock suicidally implodes.

Humans, however, have an inbuilt potential to transcend the self. On the sheerly physical level, we are not prisoners of our DNA. If nature provided us no wings, we will make them; if we lack the underwater durability of fish, we can invent machines to overcome that. In a new Ice Age we needn't crawl as far as we can, then die, like other animals; we can make fire, take the pelts of other animals, and survive. Beyond the physical, there is nearly no limit to our potential for human growth: da Vinci, Shakespeare, Dostoyevsky, Copernicus, Newton, Einstein, Buddha, Moses, Jesus, Madame Curie, Helen Keller, Dorothy Day. It is evident that the Creator intended humans to continue evolving.

Yet we are undeniably free *not* to become more and more profoundly human. We can refuse the invitation to evolve; we can act more viciously than beasts, vegetate, use others as stepping-stones. No bear can decline to act ursine, but the daily newspapers give ample testimony that humans can resist acting humanly. Here is a quite puzzling insight into the Creator! Why would the Choreographer of the Universe, the Planner of Evolution, the unquestionable Lord of Nature want to design a species that was free to *thwart* his intentions for them? Why would he freely limit his own omnipotence?

Several possibilities suggest themselves, though none of them is probative. Perhaps a free species was essential if human beings were to imitate their Creator's creativity. Perhaps the Lord of Order and Surprise is himself intrigued by surprises, good stories. Perhaps the Inventor of the giraffe, the hairy-nosed wombat, and sex has a sense of humor! And perhaps the Mind Behind It All is interested in genuine love—not the feelings and affections we share with other animals, but free commitment, which is valueless if the commitment cannot be withheld. Love is not genuine when, as with Tristan and Iseult, it is a helpless response to a love potion. Every entity in the universe—from galaxies to gluons—dumbly follows the will of its Master.

Perhaps the Master decided to experiment with a species that might offer him servitude freely and gratefully.

## FROM IMMANENT TO TRANSCENDENT—AND BACK

From what we can tell of prehistory, the original human response to a Power beyond themselves was strictly immanent, this-worldly. The supernatural spirits were locked within the waterfall, the thunder, the fire. The animism of tribes from Lapland to Samoa felt and responded to a life filled with spirits, as in the earlier quotation from Chief Seattle. Yet even pre-historic peoples had an evident belief in an afterlife, a dimension to existence beyond this one, since they buried their dead with implements and tokens for use there. Perhaps because of their own tribal experiences of hierarchical authority, they also began to suspect an Ultimate Deity, like the Native American Manitou. But the primitives' gods were to be placated and appeased, and often they could be manipulated by sacrifice, even human sacrifice.

The earliest Greek gods were chthonic, thirsty for blood, akin to and embodied in their often hostile surroundings. Later, the uneasy balance of good and bad fortune made people gradually see the gods more anthropomorphically, given to favoritism and conflict among themselves. If you can strip away the awesomeness with which classicists have veneered Homer's gods, the occupants of Olympus were really quite a dysfunc-tional family, tomcatting hither and yon, plotting behind one another's backs, shifting alliances at whim. A kind of *Dynasty* in togas.

Still later, when prosperity had given rise to the leisure requisite for unhurried philosophizing, such men as Socrates, Plato, and Aristotle found the earliest gods of their ancestors more animal-like than godlike and the Olympians less venerable than many humans. Their understanding of the Ultimate Reality was the perfection of which everything that exists in this transitory life is a weak imitation. Plato's allegory of the cave shows people chained in place, forced from birth to watch shadows on the wall before them. The shadows are thrown by a great fire behind them, which silhouettes statues carried by bearers. One prisoner escapes and confronts real trees and animals, and when he returns, he tries to convince his fellow prisoners that they have been watching shadows—of imitations—of the really real (not unlike couch potatoes in front of a television). Plato's point is that the realest real is the idea that God has of any thing (tree, horse, human). The idea is perfectly embodied in the objective thing but only imperfectly captured in our subjective ideas of the thing.

Thus, in a few hundred years, the ancients' ideas of God evolved from totally immanent to totally transcendent, shorn of any presence in the world at all, except insofar as a clockmaker is "present" in his clock. While the Greek popular culture was polytheistic, the philosophers spoke of the Ultimate Cause in the singular. It was, to all intents and purposes, deism—a monotheism as clear as that of Judaism, Christianity, and Islam, yet completely lacking their immanent-transcendent connection.

At least seen roughly, the Greeks' concept of the Deity was closer to the ideas arising in the East. The Ultimate Reality of Hinduism, Buddhism, and Taoism is totally "other," immanent only in sparks of its presence imprisoned in matter and awaiting release through meditation and often mortification of the flesh. Some of the adherents of those doctrines believe the Ultimate Reality to be personal and therefore open to communication, and union with the Deity is exactly that: an adhesion of two separate entities. Others believe the Ultimate Reality to be impersonal, and therefore union with it becomes absorption, relinquishing the individuality that was the cause of separation.

The rest of this book will consider that whole spectrum of understandings of the Mind Behind It All, their upsetting differences and their enlightening similarities. But first a word about open-mindedness.

BEYOND TOLERANCE

Once upon a time in a park in Calcutta, a group of blind men were having an outing when suddenly their nurse fell into a well and drowned. (Or ran off with her boyfriend; it hardly matters.) In near panic, the men groped around trying to find the nurse or the gate or help. "Ah!" one cried. "We've come to a wall! We can edge along it to the gate!" Another grumbled, "No, no. We're still in the woods. I can feel the stumps of the trees." Another reached up high and said, "You're right. I can feel the big palm leaves." A fourth squealed, "Ooh! I feel a spear point. Are you a guard?" A fifth man cried, "Ayee! It *is* a tree, and there's a horrible, thick snake poking out of it!" And the last man, who had gotten a bit disoriented, said, "I've got hold of a rope. Maybe it's hooked up to a bell. But, yech, it's smelly."

Each with his own impaired vision and relative point of view had come up with a quite different assessment of the same reality. Even combining and rearranging the ideas, each man was still miles away from a clear idea of the reality: an elephant. It's the same with God.

From my limited viewpoint—Western, Christian, Jesuitical, male—some religions seem to make the Power too immanent (pantheism, polytheism) because they conflict with my experience of God as often very distant and inaccessible. Others make God too transcendent (deism, the Greek philosophers) because they conflict with my experience of the numinous. However, each of the extremes acts as a corrective when my own insights and dealings with God begin to slide too close to the opposite extreme. Complementarity.

The deeper one gets into theologizing, the more God seems a cold abstraction and the study of him seems like some

kind of celestial calculus. Then immanent religions remind
me that God is not only the Uncaused First Cause—thinner
than thought, colder than calculation. God is also alive, energizing everything we see. In our eagerness for clear definitions,
we often dash right by the God who is hiding in plain sight.
Conversely, when my ideas of God get too chummy ("Jesus, m'
old buddy!"), the ideas of the more rarefied religions remind me
that God is infinitely "other," inexpressibly holy, incapable of
manipulation by bribery or blackmail or totems and amulets.

Trying to "wrap up" God, whether in a rational formula
or in a pagan idol, is as impossible as trying to comprehend the
overwhelming harmony of the universe—the dance of the
galaxies, the rhythms of the seasons, the inexhaustible variations
in nature, the complex harmonies of our bodies, the whizzing
of our minds, the airy savannas and cramped prisons of our
souls, the purpose of life, the meaning of love. The unknown—
or the barely knowable, the mysterious—will always exceed
our grasp, which is what makes true learning so exciting. Like
the blind men, we must content ourselves only with shouting
back and forth, "What does he look like from where you
stand?" Even the Hebrew Scriptures are a veritable gallery of
different images of God: the omnipotent Creator of the first
Genesis story, the God who strolls in the Garden of an evening
in the second story, the thundering, majestic God of Job, God
the husband, calling to his beloved Israel from outside her
whorehouse, God the avenger, and God the Father.

It is only by sheer accident that most of us were born into
a particular religious tradition. I suspect that most readers of
this book are probably Christian; if so, what follows—a look at
Eastern religion—may be something new. It may crack open
the understanding of God as a Dickensian bookkeeper (which
I was raised on) or of Jesus as a warm, fuzzy God who forgives
anything we do, even if we haven't the time or inclination
to drop by and apologize. Getting inside the skins of Eastern

religionists can enliven our workaday lives with the sense of an invisible but incandescent Presence all around and within us; Islam can remind us of our indebtedness and our need not merely to be sinless but also to praise.

But other readers could still be searching, reluctant to go back and reexamine the image of God they grew up with and gratefully left behind, yet hesitant to plunge into an understanding of God that is alien and strange. It can seem like giving up their citizenship (even though they fudge their taxes and don't vote) to move to a foreign country. For them, the remainder of these pages might be a chance to try the Goldilocks method: This view of God is too harsh; this view is too weak; this one is just right!

I've been an apologist for a specific religious belief for so long that it is difficult to be nonjudgmental. Yet I personally have learned more meaningful insights about praying from Buddhists than from my own religious training, more about harmony and balance from the Chinese than from my own rigidly rational theological education, more about constant contact with the Presence from Muslims than from sixty years of homilies. I still believe there is only one view that feels (more or less) just right for me, the only one whose God shared our toil, our doubt, our despair, our hope, our death. But I can still fine-tune my understanding of this Most Important Person in the Universe by shouting as I grope, "What does he look like from where you stand?"

What's more, as we shall see, the world's great religious traditions have much more in common than we might suspect. Each, without exception, for instance, has some form of the Ten Commandments. (See C. S. Lewis, *The Abolition of Man*, Appendix.) Not one of them—from Babylon to Greece, from Norse Eddas to Native American legends—lacks the equivalent of the Golden Rule, which so many wrongly believe is the specific and exclusive motto of Christianity.

In every meaning-making myth, a requirement for finding God and fulfillment is leaving home, not just the comfort or predictability of a family, but the matrix of meaning that others have forged as a haven for us until we are ready to head out in quest of our own. All the great souls left home: Buddha, Abraham, Odysseus, Psyche, Jesus, Paul, Joan of Arc, Everyman, Dorothy in *The Wizard of Oz,* and Luke Skywalker in *Star Wars.* And in every case, in every culture, the hero and heroine took possession of their own validated souls only after a sojourn in hell.

A few of us have heard resentful parents grumble, "All that money for a Catholic education, and now the kid's a Buddhist!" That's surely not the worst thing in the world, surely better than forswearing any connection to the Deity at all. A parent's purpose is to prepare children to leave home, gradually rendering themselves unnecessary and then letting the children go. They should judge their children's godliness by the vibrancy of their souls, not by their specific affiliation.

Each religion is a uniquely different connection to the sacred, to what gives ultimate coherence to one's soul life, interweaving the body-mind-spirit within the self, then outward into the web of human relationships spreading to the ends of the earth, then beyond into the transcendent Source. And the proof of the connection is not a Geiger-counter test or even a rational probe of religious beliefs but the demonstrable fullness of the adherents' lives. Each religion requires a sensitivity and vulnerability to the intangibles, which is quite difficult to evoke in our materialistic, narcissistic, hedonistic culture. All religions do not agree on the illusory value of the commonsense world, but clearly they agree to the relative unimportance of worldly accomplishment in the face of the transcendent. The elements of all religions (no matter their hierarchical structure) are the moral authority of the revelation, ritual, speculation (theology), tradition, God's sovereignty and God's grace, and mystery. And all agree with the philosopher Friedrich Schleiermacher: "Religion is the feeling of absolute dependence."

Theology is to true religion what reading Cliff's Notes is to seeing the play (or, better, acting in it). What we seek here is not just a puzzling explanation of doctrines; you have the encyclopedia if that's all you seek. Here we will try to go beyond mere tolerance of difference; we seek an understanding, an honest empathy. We want to get inside another religionist's skin and walk around in it awhile in order to find why any intelligent person would find meaning and fulfillment in what seems (at first) repellent or, at the very least, baffling. To respect, honor, and understand someone else's idea of God means not so much to understand Buddhism as to understand Buddhists, to see the world and human values as they see them. How does their belief affect their lives? Competitive religion gives way to comparative religion. The early Romans and assimilated Jews, for instance, thought that eating the body of Christ was cannibalism; the Protestant reformers in England considered the crucifix an idol. All because their preconceptions had barred them from saying, "Help me understand what *you* mean by it." (A great many parents could profit from the same lesson.)

Too few Christians realize that Jesus was ecumenical from the start. His birth was attended not only by the poor, illiterate, Jewish shepherds but also by the rich, learned, Gentile wise men. He had no problem, apparently, with a dialogue across quite varied traditions: the good Samaritan, the Samaritan woman at the well, the Syro-Phoenician woman, centurions, Nicodemus. The only ones he couldn't crack were the single-minded, exclusivist temple elders. ("Our view is the truth; thus, yours must be false. Heresy and error have no rights.")

The comparative theologian Wilfred Cantwell Smith wrote that we seek "a fellowship not of a we-they sort, but one in which some of *us* are Hindus, some of *us* are Buddhists, some of *us* are Muslims, some of *us* are Jews, some of *us* are Christians."

He might have gone further and hoped for a fellowship within one Christian denomination in which some of *us* are conservative and some of *us* are liberal, some of *us* believe in the real presence and some of *us* believe in a presence less profound. What unites all world religions—belief in the transcendent Other—is far more important than what divides us. What unites Christians—belief in a divine invasion of humanity—is more important than what we believe about Mary's virginity or the way the Trinity arranges its internal affairs. As Will Rogers wrote, "If preachers would concentrate more on our Savior's message and less on his means of arrival and departure, we'd all be a lot better off."

Unfortunately, in any organized religion, it is the hair-splitters and the bean counters who rise to the top, who take charge, not because they are imbued by the Spirit of God, but because they are efficient and get things done. Imagine if Francis of Assisi had become pope, or Gandhi had become president. Chaos! Yet Jesus made Peter the fumbler the model pope, not a theologian like John or an efficiency expert like Judas. As the king of Siam put it, "Is a puzzlement."

Therefore, in the following chapters, I will omit or give short shrift to nonessentials that might put off the ordinary reader who is not of that persuasion: reincarnation in Buddhism, polygamy and abstention from alcohol in Islam. I will try to avoid the pluralism within each tradition (for instance, in Christianity, cathedrals and Quaker meetinghouses, Trappists and Holy Rollers). I will confine the inquiry to the three major manifestations: Roman Catholic, Orthodox, and Protestant. And I will avoid the excesses of all traditions (the Inquisition, jihad, witch-hunts, snake handlers), which their originators probably would have reprehended.

When many separate teams begin to climb a mountain, they look very far apart at their base camps, but as they climb, it is still the same mountain. And when they reach the summit, they find the same God, who has been with each team all along. Then they can sit down and rest, waiting for Dr. Jastrow's scientists to catch up.

# 6

## THE EASTERN FACE

We are like a king who, falling victim to amnesia,
wanders his kingdom in tatters, not knowing who
he really is. We are like a lion cub who, having
become lost from his mother at birth, grows up by
accident among sheep and takes to grazing and
bleating like them, assuming that he too is a sheep.
We are like a lover who, dreaming, searches the
world in despair for his beloved, oblivious to the
fact that she is lying by his side.

—HUSTON SMITH, *THE RELIGIONS OF MAN*

All religions grow out of a sacramental basis; that is, they
begin from an experience of the holy in the here and now, a
sacred transcendence whose presence issues an ethical call to
organize one's life within a context larger than the everyday. The
religions of both East and West began with personifications of
that felt power in anthropomorphic gods, but with time and
reflection, a more rarefied Deity emerged. The Western mind
has been deeply imbued by the clearheaded Greeks; it practices
an intellectual rigor intolerant of fuzzy ideas or contradictory
reasoning. Far more like the practitioners of modern science, the
Eastern mind is comfortable with ambiguity, paradox, or what
would seem to a westerner outright contradiction. One is tempted
to suspect that the Eastern understanding of God might be
closer to the real thing. According to legend, Thomas Aquinas

said at his death that before the face of the Reality, all his work was straw.

## HINDUISM

The essence of Hinduism, the earliest of the Eastern religions, is oneness. In fact, there is no word for religion in Hindi, since the transcendent connection is not compartmentalized into one time in the week or a particular sacred space but pervades every crevice and corner of life. Every object, every person, every space is saturated with the sacred.

Two thousand years before Christ, sages penned Vedas (as in the Latin *video,* "I perceive and understand"), long poems filled with a fabulous menagerie of gods and demons more exotic than the Greeks' but just as unpredictable. Each was a personification of some aspect of human life—water, prayer, cattle—roughly comparable to the Christian pantheon of patron saints. The Hindu scriptures, unlike the Bible and the Koran, are not strictly speaking revelations from a personal God to a privileged individual messenger. Rather, they are an understanding of human life mediated from some generalized spiritual agency (like the Force of *Star Wars*) to an unknown sage. Over time, ritual sacrifice became the connection to these divine powers; as the rituals became more and more complicated, the role of the priests became more focal in this most important element of people's lives. The priests became the first caste: the Brahmans.

Gradually, this nonspeculative, primitive Vedic religion gave way to a more sophisticated understanding of the divine and human. As in Greece, it arose out of skepticism and speculation that led to the subordination of all the lesser gods to one Ultimate Deity. Despite other Vedic hymns celebrating lesser gods, one declares:

> The gods were born after this world's creation:
> Then who can know whence it has arisen?

As the Upanishad ("to sit down with") poems began to replace the simpler Vedas, the power of priests and the exclusive connection to the gods through sacrifice began to give way to a less ritualized, more interiorized sense of linkage with the supernatural. The sages began to see that behind each god in the bewildering pantheon, there was a spiritual reality (roughly similar to Plato's divine ideas). Each of the varied gods was, in fact, just a different manifestation and incarnation of the one Ultimate Reality, each embodying in a symbolic way the many facets of the conflict between good and evil, and each a face of the One: the Brahman.

## The Brahman and the Atman

*Brahman* (literally, "the ever growing") is a neuter noun and not a proper name. At least in the Upanishads, God is incapable of deliberate action and therefore is not a person but rather the essence of the world soul within all things. The Brahman is one and many, becoming and unchanging, personal and impersonal, fullness and emptiness, good and evil. The Brahman, in fact, is beyond words, beyond even *being* and *nonbeing. Brahman* exists—but even that word fails. Unlike the God of the Bible, the Brahman is not a moral being or a lawgiver. It is beyond even good and evil.

God is utter reality, utter awareness, utter bliss. For the Eastern mind, trying to trap God into words is like trying to lasso the wind. Brahman exists in everything, like separate bubbles at the bottom of kettle rising to be absorbed within themselves. Again unlike the religions originating from Abraham, prayer is not a connection to a divine Person—Yahweh or Jesus or Allah—but rather a connection to the divine within and beyond the individual. To use a crude analogy, it is more like a connection to a transcendent Generator of Life Energy.

The Atman (again neuter) is the individual correlative of the Brahman, the innermost self of each individual. The world soul and the individual soul are one. In the West, the soul is separate from and subordinate to God; in the East, both God and the individual are one-and-the-same substance and on the same level. The key sentence in Hinduism is *Tat tvam asi* (literally, "That thou to be"). Atman is Brahman in the approximately similar and mystifying way that matter is energy. The soul of each person is the world soul. Equivalently, each Hindu claims what Jesus claimed: "I and the Father are one." It is akin to Jesus' prayer at the Last Supper in John's Gospel: "I gave them the same glory you gave me, so that they may be one, just as you and I are one: I in them and you in me, so that they may be completely one" (John 17:22–23, TEV). The essence of Hinduism is realizing that oneness.

Thus, Hinduism is a monistic (one entity includes all) pantheism (all is God).

Within the Brahman there is nonetheless a kind of trinity, not three persons in one God but three aspects of the same God: Brahma, Shiva, and Vishnu. Brahma is the Creator who continually brings rebirth to the cosmos, just as to individual souls in their endless reincarnations, out of the used up "stuff" of a previous cosmos. Even though the assertion is three thousand years old, it is not unlike the scientific speculation that this universe was once a singularity, infinitely dense and nonextended, that exploded and might implode back, only to explode again. But Brahma has better things to do than interfere in everyday living. His two other facets are more significant.

Shiva, the Destroyer, accounts for the aspect of God captured in that age-old question "How could a good God . . . ?" Shiva is a many-sided fellow, weird, fierce, fond of graveyards, always pictured with a necklace of skulls. But he is also ascetic, with matted hair and a body covered with ashes. Shiva kills the god of love with a glance, yet he is also the Lord of the Dance, keeping the cosmos moving.

Vishnu is the Protector, the bright side of God, the savior who appears on earth in active god-figures—avatars, human incarnations—age after age. He assures that nothing is truly destroyed, since sheer Being—the Brahman—is the only true reality, everywhere and always. It is important to realize the difference between these incarnations and the Christian doctrine of the incarnation of the Second Person of the Trinity. In that doctrine, the Word literally became flesh, fully human and yet still fully divine. In the Hindu doctrine, the Shiva or Vishnu facet of God merely puts on human guise in order to deal directly with humankind.

## The Human Condition

Some key terms are essential to understand the Hindu beliefs about the evolution of the Atman (the divine self) into the Brahman (the One). The first is *samsara:* continual rebirth after death into a new, more (or less) purified level of being. Thus developed the notion of *caste,* each new level signifying not only a nobler, more privileged worthiness but also a greater responsibility to purify the self even more fully for yet another advancement (or slippage) in a subsequent life. The determinant of one's direction in a subsequent life is *karma:* the record of one's moral life and its consequences. Just as in Christianity, "as you sow, so shall you reap." It is important to realize that to the Hindu, misdeeds do not bring punishment from a moral God; that's simply the way things are. Violate the right ways, the underlying order of the universe, and you will pay the price in your subsequent life. Therefore, the individual takes complete responsibility for his or her future lives; there is no chance or accidents, no lame excuses. The moral code is *dharma:* righteousness, duty, honesty, decency, respect, and care for others. But the code varies as you ascend the ladder of castes, increasing in demands. The final goal is *moksha:* escape from the round of samsara, beyond the highest (Brahman) caste, into the world soul.

To understand the oneness is not to be saved but to be liberated. Just as in Christianity Jesus is the incarnation of God, so too is the Atman in each individual. As St. Paul wrote, "I live now, not I, but Christ lives in me." A person's true self is divinity; the everyday self is maya, which is usually translated "illusion." But that is not quite true or fair, and it gives rise to a radical misunderstanding of Hinduism. The everyday world is not quite illusion, but it is real only insofar as dreams are real or the patterns of light and shadow on a movie screen (or the wall of Plato's cave) are real. Again, consider the insights of modern science: The chair that supports your weight is not really solid at all but aswarm with galaxy upon galaxy of moving parts—and most of it is empty space. Reality is relative only to your present ability to perceive it.

### Ways to God

There are only two basic approaches to human life: the path of desire and the path of renunciation. Most people, by nature or by nurture, presume there is only the path of desire, not only fulfilling basic needs like food, clothing, and shelter, but also "going for it with all the gusto you can." Pleasure and worldly success seem the unquestionable goals of any sane person. The students I teach (all of them victims of what they call eleven years of Christian brainwashing) are resolutely and impregnably convinced that human fulfillment comes from money, fame, sex, and power. "What is he worth?" is merely another way of saying, "How much does he make?" It's almost impossible to persuade them that pleasure is not wicked, just too narrow and fleeting to fulfill them. They can't yet sense the limits of happiness: unexpected pain, frustration at thwarted desires, boredom, finitude. Nor can they sense that the pursuit of happiness in material things is bottomless: Scrooge can never get enough, and most adults are looking for fulfillment in dolls and trains, children's toys. Only when a person arrives at that understanding of life's illusions is he or she ready for the path of renunciation. Until that point, the Hindu sage will leave you alone.

Renunciation need be neither negative nor pessimistic. Rather, it is a sacrifice of an objectively trivial security for an awareness that is more deeply life giving, like a mother in labor. One submits the self to the larger community, no longer to dominate but to be used, not to triumph but merely to do one's best. But even that wears out. What we really want is infinity. As Augustine of the West said, "Our hearts are restless till they rest in Thee." Our true goal is to touch the white-hot center of every life: Atman, the infinite buried under the almost impenetrable load of distractions and seeming values.

*Yoga* comes from the same Indo-European root as the word *yoke,* a means both to unite and to subdue and control, leading the self into integration with the All. Hinduism is most adaptable to the proclivities of individuals. (In fact, some claim that there are as many Hinduisms as there are Hindus.) One yoga outlines a way to God for reflective people who find God through study, another for affectionate people who find God in loving, still another for active people who connect to God in serving, and finally another for contemplative people who are at ease with meditation.

1. The yoga of knowing is for those whose temperament is philosophical. It calls for shifting thought from the passing part of one's life to the eternal in it, withdrawing and observing life as an intent witness, seeking the true actor who spends most of the day behind a mask.

2. The yoga of loving, unlike the first way, seeks not to perceive one's identity with the Divine but to feel it, without either the Brahman or the Atman absorbing the other. One sees everything in life as a matchmaker to God, seeking to love God as one would love a parent, friend, lover, child.

3. The yoga of working moves through the everyday tasks not just from economic need but also from psychological need. Without entering a monastery, one can fling the self into work as a vehicle for transcendence,

lose oneself in order to find oneself, as athletes lose themselves in performance—yet never feeling so vibrantly a self as within it. Every action performed in the service of God is energized by the God-presence within (Atman) if one does each task as if it is the only thing one had to do in a lifetime.

4. The yoga of meditating seeks actually to experience the Divine within by willed introversion—quiescent but alert, receptive and not passive, the body and mind disconnected and at peace—in order to become literally absorbed in God.

The Hindus can teach us much about God and our connection to God: Compared to children, we are adults; compared to saints, we are children.

## BUDDHISM

This segment will find me reaching for the thesaurus more often, looking for synonyms for *bewildering* and *daunting*. Some of Buddhism's most crucial insights pretty much defy simplification without falsification. Moreover, its methodology—with its Three Characteristics, Four Aggregates, Six Perfections, Nine Incompatibles, Ten Recollections (which are only a few of the schematics)—can make Buddhism seem a rabbit warren of concepts, enough to send the rational Western mind spinning. But I will try to simplify, at least to whet some appetites.

### A Hindu Protestantism

Buddhism began as a reaction against Hindu excesses, each element of which had gotten out of hand. Castes had become cruelly exclusive and exploitative, rituals were available only for a price, speculation had become nit-picking, tradition had made ancient Sanskrit the language of ritual (though the people didn't understand it), and mystery had degraded to superstition. There are not a few parallels to the Christian church of the sixteenth century and to the Roman Catholic Church during the first half of the twentieth century.

To counteract these excesses, the Buddha evolved a worldview and a pragmatic system of self-discipline that had (1) no authorities, caste, or patriarchal sexism—a democratic belief that forced each individual back to his or her own thinking, (2) no elaborate ritual, (3) no speculative theology but rather a focus on the individual soul, (4) no tradition, which shackles growth (whatever ritual there was would be in the language of the people), (5) no salvation from outside one's own sovereign soul, and (6) no miracles, shortcuts, or intervention by gods—a rejection of the Vedic gods, who were now superseded by those who had achieved nirvana and Buddhahood, not by divine right, but by their own relentless pursuit of enlightenment. Buddha neither accepted nor rejected a personal God outside the human dimension.

The latter may be the most difficult concept for a westerner to grasp. There is no room in Buddhism for a Supreme Being as we conceive of him: creator, manipulator, a God who hears and helps. It is very much a do-it-yourself religion, and it is a strain to say that Buddhism is even "religion" in our accepted sense of a connection to a Person. However, it certainly is a connection to an Entity (unfocused as that might be) that transcends space and time.

The Hindu Upanishads strive to eliminate all desires except the desire for God; in contrast, Buddhism strives to eliminate that very desire for God more than any other, since that is the desire from which all other inhibiting desires spring. The Upanishads see the soul as a mango pit wrapped in leaves, and when you unwrap the final leaf, there is the pit—the self-soul. Buddhists see the soul as an onion, and when you peel back the last leaf, there is nothing. Unsettling as that concept is, we can recall the views of some modern scientists who say that when you burrow down to the inside of the most primitive atomic particle, you will find nonextended energy.

## Siddhartha Gautama

When people asked the Buddha what he was, he answered simply, "I am awake." The Sanskrit root of the word *Buddha* is *budh*, both "to wake up" and "to know." He was a man awakened from the dream of everyday life and the cycles of recurring lives.

In about 560 B.C., Siddhartha Gautama left home. He had been egregiously spoiled by his father, who had been told by an oracle that the boy would be either a prince to unite all India or a wise ascetic who would liberate the world. His father had shielded him in every way, lavishing on him every pleasure, protecting him from the slightest anxiety (as most parents hope to do), and thus screening him from adult life in the world we have. In varying accounts, Gautama eluded his father's protectiveness and discovered the Four Passing Sights: a man sick, a man decrepit, a man dead, and a man dedicated to a life of self-denial and begging. In puzzlement, he retired from his life of pleasure to probe the causes and the remedies for human suffering.

Every philosopher begins with suffering: Why aren't things as they should be? If you haven't begun your philosophizing there, you haven't begun. Gautama (at his father's behest) had tried the way of unchecked hedonism; then after his encounter with suffering, he tried unmitigated mortification and self-denial. At length, he settled on the Middle Way, avoiding the excesses of either indulgence or asceticism. He decided on rigorous thought and meditation.

Finally, he sat immovable in the wilderness under the *bo*, "wisdom," tree—which has its obvious parallels in other religious understandings: Moses in the desert of Midian before encountering the burning bush, Jesus in the wilderness wrestling

with Satan, Mohammed entombed in his cave. It seems a
constant in most of the great religions that only on a sojourn
through hell does one finds one's soul. Gautama eventually
broke through into a sense of unity with all living things. He sat
in the wilderness for seven weeks of rapture, a feeling akin to
the Christian sense of resurrection-in-life, a total turnabout of
his worldly values, an utter rebirth.

When he woke from his ecstatic trance, he faced the
ultimate question: How could one possibly communicate what
can be discovered only for oneself? His only response was, "Some
will understand." And hundreds of millions for the last two
millennia have. For nearly fifty years, Gautama—now an emer-
gent Buddha, a bodhisattva (ready for nirvana but willing to
delay that for the sake of others)—trudged across India with his
message. He founded an order of monks, who spent nine months
a year preaching and used the rainy season for retreat and
prayer. In about 480 B.C., he died and, presumably, was assumed
into the Ultimate Reality. Like Socrates, he seems to have been
a man of cool head and warm heart, and like Jesus, he was
impervious to caste or sexism. Throughout his life, he refused
to be revered as some kind of god.

## Doctrine

Buddha saw that the essence of human life is to suffer in a
transitory world. Death is not the greatest fear; far greater is
the fear of rebirth into yet another grinding round of suffering.
He saw that speculation does nothing whatever to relieve
suffering; therefore, he offered an existential explanation of the
causes of suffering and a pragmatic program to cure it. He
accepted the Hindu concepts of samsara (reincarnation), karma
(the effect of moral life on one's future life), dharma (a guide for
moral behavior), and moksha (ultimate deliverance, which
Buddhists call nirvana)—but from a completely revamped
perspective from Hinduism's.

*The Buddha.*   Who or what is the Buddha (a title, not a proper name)? There are three understandings:

1. **The historical man Siddhartha Gautama,** the discoverer and prime exemplar of the path to nirvana. In Theravada Buddhism, he is the only true subject of the predicate *Buddha.*

2. **The bodhisattva,** an embodiment in human form of the Buddha truths. This person qualifies for nirvana now but willingly defers it in order to lead others along the path to the truth.

3. **The cosmic Buddha,** an otherworldly being of infinite wisdom and compassion. But this being is not God as Christians think of God, the creator and sustainer. The cosmic Buddha simply is, although in at least one sect, he is the cosmic Lord whose body is the cosmos. And all Buddhists accept Maitreya, the Buddha-yet-to-come, who is quite like the Christian notion of the second coming of Christ.

The usual statues of the Buddha and the crucifix distill the essence of the two beliefs and hint at a rough idea of the contrasts. Buddha is usually seated in a lotus position with his eyes closed, focused in self-enclosed concentration. Jesus on the cross most often has wide eyes and gaping mouth, and as Chesterton said, his four-beamed cross seems to reach the four corners of the world. The statues also suggest the difference in the understanding of prayer: Christianity reaches for a connection between two discrete persons ("My God, my God, why have you abandoned me?"); Buddhism reaches inward to a source of essential power. The great Christian mystics open their souls unhesitatingly so that God might enter and ravish them; the Buddhist mystics close around their own essence and blind themselves to all else but the God already within.

*Nirvana.*   Nirvana is another puzzling idea. Its root word means "to extinguish," which suggests (at least partially wrongly) that achievement of fulfillment is a sort of soul suicide and that Buddhism is basically an atheist humanism. Yet it is not annihilation but bliss, and if there is bliss, there must unarguably be a subject to experience that bliss. Invoking again the principle of complementarity, nirvana is both absorption and separateness, the indescribable final good, bliss uncontaminated by attachment or dependence. Nirvana is a concept no more susceptible to comprehension than the eternal experience of the Christian beatific vision (which seems to many a pretty static form of happiness). If indifference to a personal Creator is atheism, Buddha was an atheist, and Buddhism is not strictly speaking a religion. Yet that constraint forces the Eastern mind to conform to Western expectations of the limits of reality.

*The soul.*   The Buddha's idea of the soul is yet another befuddlement for the Western mind. He denied a spiritual entity that retained separateness at the ultimate release, yet he never denied the this-worldly transmigration of the soul from one life cycle to the next, like the same flame passed from one torch to the next. It is (confusedly) clear that Buddha says an enlightened one does not live on, yet it is just as (confusedly) clear that he would deny that the enlightened ceases to exist. The key, I think, as we saw with Brahman, is the limits that all humans, Western and Eastern, put on the word *exist.* Either something exists or it doesn't; one can't "sort of exist" any more than one can be "sort of pregnant" or "sort of dead." The Western mind holds that the Divine (personal or impersonal) does exist, but in a manner only remotely analogous to the way humans or cattle or vegetation or even ideas exist. The Eastern mind holds that those who have achieved total fulfillment have gone beyond any predicates, beyond even "He is real." Thus, those who attain Buddhahood do not "live on" in the individualized form forced on them by each rebirth. What lives on is the essence that has undergone each transformation.

The best explanation I have found is that it is not the droplet that is absorbed in the ocean; it is the ocean that enters the droplet. (Those with active right lobes might understand.)

*The Four Noble Truths.*   The kernel of the Buddha's doctrine is the Four Noble Truths:

1. Life is suffering. Even joy is disguised pain. Not to mention the obvious cases in which suffering is patent, suffering (at least in the broadest sense of giving up something good in the hope of something better) is unarguably an even greater part of our lives than most of us are aware of. We have become so used to it, it no longer appears to be suffering but merely the way things are. Getting out of the warm cocoon of the blankets is, in that broadest sense, suffering. So is working, learning, loving, growing. That's why so little growing happens.

2. The cause of suffering is selfish desire, isolating the self from the One and from others who are fellow facets of the same Ultimate Reality. Even together, we are as isolated in the prisons of our flesh as patients in a mental ward.

3. The end of suffering comes with release from the narrow limits of self-interest. Few of the great world religions would argue with that concept, though they would surely argue about the means to achieve that release.

4. The Buddha way (dharma) to that release is the Eightfold Path.

*The Eightfold Path.*   The Eightfold Path is not a cure from outside but a system of habit formation from within. Before embarking on that path, the aspirant must associate with one further along (as with twelve-step programs), with the understanding that spiritual health is as contagious as spiritual disease. The first two steps describe the human situation; the second three direct proper moral behavior; the final three are a program of thought control pointed toward enlightenment.

1. **Right knowledge.** As with the first of the twelve steps, the basic Buddhist movement is a realization that life is indeed out of joint and that for now one is helpless to deal with it alone and needs instruction.

2. **Right aspiration.** One needs determination to transcend one's separateness, which means renunciation of enclosure in sensuality, malice, and vindictiveness. Negatively, the Buddhist should be incapable of murder, theft, sexual impurity, lies, hedonism, partiality, hatred, stupidity, and fear.

3. **Right speech.** The first step toward wisdom is to call a thing by its right name and not to call it anything at all unless one is certain that it is true (thus the Buddhist's hesitancy to use the word *exist* about entities with whom no one can have direct contact).

4. **Right behavior.** The five precepts of behavior are almost identical with the latter Ten Commandments: Do not kill, steal, lie, be unchaste, or drink intoxicants.

5. **Right livelihood.** One's occupation should promote life rather than erode it; earning a living is a means, not an end. A doctor, for instance, may kill viruses only because they are a threat to a greater good.

6. **Right effort.** Overcoming one's weaknesses and evolving good habits is a strenuous business. The will must control the body and mind; slow and steady wins the race.

7. **Right mindfulness.** One must see everything in perspective, as it really is, rigorously separating the authentic from the trivial.

8. **Right absorption.** Eventually, even logical thought itself is annihilated. As nirvana is the distillation of perfection, concentration is the essence of the path to perfection—a concept that, in a world of incessant distractions, is repellent to many, yet desirable to the few who honestly say, "There must be more than this."

## The Split

Since there are so many Buddhist splinter sects, we can consider only the two major ones: Theravada, the Smaller Vehicle that aims at the mind and accommodates relatively few, and Mahayana, the Larger Vehicle that aims at the heart and accommodates many.

Theravada is a path primarily for monks; the laity pursue improvement of their karma by supporting the monks and feeding them. Ritual is reprehensible since it adds illusion to what is already illusion, like the semisuperstitious practices in Catholicism before Vatican II that promised indulgences for so many days of uninterrupted rosaries. The members of this stricter and therefore more exclusive sect strive not merely to be upright souls but also to become saints. Theravada is more or less concentrated in the countries of Southeast Asia—Myanmar, Cambodia, Laos, Thailand, Sri Lanka. In some countries, a quarter of the males wear the saffron gown and undergo the monks' practices, at least for a time, just as Mormons give a percentage of their time to missionary service or as the sons of medieval and Renaissance nobles learned for a while "the higher things" in monasteries.

Mahayana is primarily for laypeople, who are counseled by a guru or a bodhisattva. This sect expands the doctrines of the great Buddha-heavens and many heavenly Buddhas, but this segment of Buddhism, which predominates in India, China, Japan, and Korea, is more readily accessible to westerners looking for a larger perspective.

## Meditation and Discipline

Like the proliferation of offshoot doctrines, there are uncountable suggestions for the mind control and discipline needed to center the self. The best known is Zen, coming through the Japanese sensibility (in China, *Ch'an;* in India, *jhana*). It is a system of pragmatic means to short-circuit the intrusions of the body and the calculating intelligence to achieve active contemplation of the Buddha (the Awakened) at the heart of oneself. But prayer, study, and discipline are only "the tracks of the bird the hunter pursues, not the bird itself." One finds that connection through intuitional insight, not through disciplined reasoning or meticulous instruction. Achieving it is remotely like those "Aha!" moments that lesser folk know in numinous encounters, only more protracted.

There are two fundamental components of the Buddhist ethic: wisdom and compassion—the mother love that puts others' welfare before one's own. But like abstention from self-indulgence, compassion is a handmaiden to wisdom. Buddhism is not a doctrine of salvation by works, since moral conduct alone doesn't guarantee enlightenment.

Reading Zen writings is often, for the westerner, like reading *Alice in Wonderland:* bewildering dialogues, obscure puzzles and paradoxes, flagrant contradictions and non sequiturs. When you ask a proficient, "What is Zen?" he might hand you a ball or give you a slap. These riddles are intended to short-circuit the rational intelligence with which we try to figure everything out, stay on top of things, maintain control. What is so dear to westerners is anathema to the Zen ascetic, who has a deep-seated distrust of words that camouflage, oversimplify, or sell short the multifaceted truth in the name of comforting certitude. (Recall what I said before about trying to rationalize love or humor.)

One wonders if Francis of Assisi and Thérèse of Lisieux, Teilhard de Chardin and Albert Einstein might find much to share with the heavenly Buddhas.

## CONFUCIANISM

In the millennium before Christ, Chinese religion was a blend of nature worship, in which spirits were invoked and appeased, and ancestor worship, in which family members who had died were petitioned for intervention. The chief god—*Ti'an,* "Heaven"—was not so much a personal being as a universal moral principle by which kings were mandated or deposed. The political ethos into which Confucius was born was a chaos of social anarchy, self-interest, customs such as abandoning female infants, almost continual petty warfare, and mass executions of the conquered. The young Confucius might find similar challenges today.

### *Confucius*

The name *Confucius* was Latinized by early Jesuit missionaries from the name *K'ung-Fu-tzu,* "Kung, the Master" (551–479 B.C.), who was born in a minor Chinese province to a family of the lesser nobility. Since his father died when the boy was very young, the boy had to make his own way alone, and he became a sage and scholar by dint of curiosity and perseverance.

Like Socrates, there was nothing otherworldly about him. He was a good man but hardly prepossessing, yet, like Socrates, he became a one-man university who taught by conversing. His sayings, collected after his death in *The Analects,* seem often no more than homey moral maxims expressing what is required of the ideal gentleman (in the British sense), yet there is a much more profound system of moral thought undergirding them. Confucius was a classicist who immersed himself in the ancient Chinese texts, unearthing, refining, preserving what he believed the best of ancient culture, forming a kind of template for the rulers who could save his province and his country from moral implosion.

He tried for his considerable lifetime to secure some post where he might test out his theories, but year after year he failed because no leader was looking for an adviser who was not a dishonest, ruthless flatterer. As with the prophet Jeremiah, the audience was small for a man who told leaders, flatly and incessantly, that if they wanted to govern well, they should stop being selfish and cruel. Instead Confucius wandered, trying to find ways by any means possible (street talks, entertainment, education) to inculcate virtue, an *inner* moral imperative that would lessen the need for so many ineffective laws.

Like Socrates and Plato, Confucius was a thwarted statesman who attracted idealistic young men to his centers of learning and began training political leaders (probably no more than seventy) who scattered at his death to become teachers themselves and at times even government officials. At the unification of the separate Chinese kingdoms into the empire under the Han dynasty, such a far-flung governmental apparatus needed administrators, and the Confucian school was ready-made. By the first century B.C., Confucianism was the official guide for political and religious practice. Its effectiveness lay in shifting access to governmental power from uncritically inherited nobility to acquired ability.

## Doctrine

If the Western mind would consider that Buddhism has a tenuous claim on the word *religion,* the claim of Confucianism is even thinner, and studying it might seem impertinent in a book about seeking God. It is no more an organized, institutional religion than is Socratism or Platonism. There is no explicit doctrine or dogma. In no sense was Confucianism ever considered "divine revelation." Yet there is certainly a transcendent dimension to it that deserves consideration. In the sayings of Confucius recorded in *The Analects,* he clearly and often speaks of the will of Heaven (which implies at least some kind of purposeful subject) and of the otherworldly survival of ancestors (which necessitates a real dimension to life transcending the here and now). This is not crystal-clear affirmation of a personal God; Hitler preached that Providence wanted society hierarchized by the pigments of people's skins. Yet Confucius did say, "He who offends the gods has no one to whom to pray," and his moral doctrine was surely of the noblest order.

Confucianism has three focal concepts: Ti'an (Heaven), Jen (Goodness), and Tao (the Way).

*Ti'an (Heaven).*   Where the Western mind itches to measure in foot-candles the distance of each saint from the divine throne, the Eastern mind is content (and perhaps closer to the truth) with something much more unfocused. Depending on the disciple interpreting the Master, Ti'an (Heaven) could be either a vital and purposeful (therefore personal) power who generates the moral law or an impersonal moral force, a cosmic counterpart of the human ethical sense. In some passages of *The Analects,* Confucius seems to confess the same implicit trust in the will of Heaven as we find in the Hebrew psalmist. If a ruler violates the will of Heaven, he can expect the same treatment meted out to David and Ahab.

But it does seem clear that Confucius found Heaven simply "given" and felt no need to probe its metaphysical properties. He was far more concerned with finding ways to have the will of Heaven replicated here on earth.

*Jen (Goodness).*   Jen is the will of Heaven. All that is true, right, and proper is the fundamental character of the Supreme Being and thus normative for upright human beings. Unlike many of the Christian Protestant reformers, Confucius assumed the basic goodness of human nature. Later his disciple Mencius (Meng-tsu) attempted to validate that assumption more empirically: If any normal person saw a child teetering at the lip of a well, he or she would instinctively react to save the child—not to attain the approval of the parents or neighbors, nor to escape blame for not acting, but quite simply because the child and the onlooker are basically good.

*Tao (the Way).*     Tao is the Way to Heaven, parallel to Buddhist dharma, that Confucius distilled from his study of the Chinese classics, searching for instances of those who were unarguably good, benevolent, compassionate—and by that very means effective. Therefore, the Way to Heaven is not through codified laws but by the contemplation of people who were in fact humanly fulfilled.

Confucius's attitude toward ritual is worth considering. More important than meticulous performance is the attitude of the worshiper. "If I am not present at the sacrifices," he said, "there is no sacrifice." Moreover, he held that ritual should err always to the side of the spare rather than the lavish. On the one hand, the ritual ought not be merely pro forma; on the other, it ought not to be a performance, which many in other religious traditions could well take to heart.

The cult of ancestors, which Roman Catholic authorities condemned as idolatry when they received word of it from the first missionaries to China, is no more idolatry than the Christian communion of saints. It is a belief that those who have gone before are still part of our family. At death, the name of the deceased is inscribed on a plaque and put in a place of reverence in the home, sometimes for generations, and then ensconced in a temple. At special times, like birth, marriage, or a new opportunity, the family gathers around the tablet and table, offering food, incense, flowers, and candles, asking for a blessing, especially on the eve of a new year.

Whether Confucius held for a personal God or not, his ethical humanism certainly calls on a heavenly power for its validation, and it certainly has led to a moral holiness in many. The most distinctive feature of Confucianism is that it teaches not by laws but by persons. "If the ruler himself is upright, all will go well, even though he does not give orders." There are two kinds of authority: external authority—which is bestowed, inherited, or captured, often by those morally unworthy to wield it—and internal authority achieved by study, reflection, and practice, which lends power to its possessors even if they hold no official office at all, as with Confucius. Like the Aristotelian ethics of habitual virtue, we learn to be brave by acting bravely. Our attitude is at the root of all our actions. "A gentleman takes as much effort to discover what is right as lesser men take to discover what will pay."

When asked, "Is there any single saying that one can act upon all day and every day?" the Master replied, "Never do to others what you would not like them to do to you." Five hundred years before Jesus.

## TAOISM

As a religion, Taoism hardly qualifies. Its adherents who do engage in ritual cult usually restrict themselves to what the greater world religions would consider superstition: mediums, shamans, exorcists, and so forth. It is not a unified or even clearly defined movement. But Taoism's philosophy—or more accurately its attitude—is worth consideration. If Confucianism is yang, "masculine," Taoism is yin, "feminine." Confucianism is rational and analytical; Taoism is intuitive and sees things whole.

### Lao-tzu and the Tao

Lao-tzu ("the Old Master" or "the Old Boy") was a contemporary of Confucius, though about fifty years older, and there is a story that Confucius once met with him and said, "Now I have met a dragon." Little is known of Lao-tzu, and a great deal of what is known is challenged. But there is general agreement that he wrote a large part of the *Tao Te Ching*, "The Way and Its Power," which may have been later completed and edited by another hand.

The Tao (pronounced "Dow") signifies both the Ultimate Reality and the way toward achieving union with it (neuter).

The Tao is the transcendent ground of all existence, an unchanging unity underlying all shifting varieties, the basic "stuff," primal and formless, as utterly simple yet potent as the modern scientists' singularity. In chapter 25 of the *Tao Te Ching:*

> There was something undifferentiated and yet
>     complete,
> Which existed before heaven and earth.
> Soundless and formless, it depends on nothing and
>     does not change.
> It operates everywhere and is free from danger.
> It may be considered the Mother of the Universe.
> I do not know its name; I call it Tao.

The Tao is not only transcendent but also immanent, the impersonal energy beneath all energies, a reality found in all things but identifiable in none. The Tao is not far from Bergson's *elan vital,* the dynamic creative force at the root of all existence, or the unfocused Force of *Star Wars.* It is a unitive force beyond rational analysis, nor is there any possibility of communication with it. "The Tao that can be conceived is not the Tao."

## Doctrine

The only doctrine in Taoism is that there are no doctrines. Its basic insight is that of all other religions: We are not God! Its message is to yield to the Tao, to be open, free, easy, adaptive, loose, serenely confident. The truest worship is within our attitude: Go with the flow, yield to the Tao rather than try to dominate it or control it or manipulate it with unheard prayers. This attitude couldn't be further from the world-beater's dream of making it or the entrepreneur's quest to dominate nature and subdue it and render it profitable.

That yielding, as we saw earlier when we first considered complementarity, is symbolized in the endless fluctuations back and forth in the yin and yang, a circle (the infinite line) bisected by a wavy line, one side white (the masculine yang), one black (the feminine yin), yet each with a spot of the other color capsulated within it. It is a perfect whole, fluctuating yet balanced. There is no way to say that it is a white circle with a black curve, or vice versa. It is a synthesis of yang (hot, dry, active, light, movement, fire, heaven, male) and yin (cool, moist, receptive, dark, rest, water, earth, female). A total balance, a synthesis of rest and movement.

This idea is in direct contrast with Persian Zoroastrianism, which saw the opposites within human life as contradictory and in open conflict and in order to explain them postulated two gods, Ahura Mazda, the god of light and goodness, and Ahriman, the god of darkness and evil. By various routes, that reassuringly clear-cut division crept into the great Western religions, Judaism, Christianity, and Islam: God and the devil, exploiters and exploited, either/or, religious and secular, science and faith, spirit and flesh—all in constant antagonism.

Rather, Taoism is more/less (at the moment) a bipolar relationship of opposites, the form of one side of the circle giving form to the other but always gradually balancing out. It echoes the Hegelian dialectic in which the current state of affairs (the thesis) is gradually confronted by its opposite (the antithesis) and over time works out a compromise (the synthesis—which itself becomes a new thesis). It is also mirrored in the third law of motion: For every action there is an equal and opposite reaction. In human affairs, the easeful spirit of Taoism in the face of this flux is captured in the cliché "This too shall pass." The person in agony (who has achieved serenity and the long view) knows that the agony will someday end. Conversely, the proud exploiters fail to realize that the seeds of their downfall are lurking within their own arrogance.

The clearest advice that Lao-tzu offers about our attitude toward the Tao is to be "humble as water." We cannot know the

Tao; we can only be absorbed and ruled by it, as water yields to the storm and to the calm. "Do without any ado."

That oneness with the Tao emerges in the great Chinese tapestries all of us have seen, soaring mountains and clouds, with the human elements, like bridges and houses and people, small yet secure, having a small place in the overall picture—but nonetheless a place, an "at home." It shows intuitive harmony between nature (savage or serene) and one's own humanity.

"Bide in silence, and the radiance of the spirit shall come in and make its home."

The climbers on the western face could learn much from the climbers on the eastern face.

# 7

## THE WESTERN FACE

In the beginning, when God created the universe,
the earth was formless and desolate. The raging
ocean that covered everything was engulfed in total
darkness, and the Spirit of God was moving over
the water. Then God commanded, "Let there be
light"—and light appeared.

—GENESIS I:I−3, TEV

### JUDAISM

All three major Western religions are joined in Judaism
at their roots. All Jews, Christians, and Muslims are spiritual
Semites. The Jews' way of looking at the relationship between
the transcendent Presence and the immanent Presence and
our human relationship with him tinges later developments and
branchings from that Source. God is the Unique One, and all
else in the universe is his creation, subservient and beholden to
him. One sentence encapsulates the heart of Judaism and is said
by fervent Jews every day and tacked on their doorposts in a
mezuzah: the Shema.

*Shema Ysroel Adonoy elohaynu Adonoy echod.*
Hear, O Israel, the Lord our God, the Lord is One.

Judaism (and its two later derivations, Christianity and Islam) is an ethical monotheism. It refuses absolutely to give even possibility to any other entity claiming divine status. Unlike the religions of the East, there might be room for angels and saints but no other gods, however minor and dependent. Unlike the Olympians and many of the earlier Eastern gods, Yahweh is not capricious, amoral, or indifferent but steady, just, and merciful, intimately involved even in the everyday. Also quite unlike Eastern beliefs, the God of Israel is a personal Deity who carries on a loving relationship with his people and, in the case of Israel, even enters into a unique covenant with them that can be understood only by analogy to a marriage.

The idea of the chosen people often seems to outsiders like some kind of dismissively exclusive, even smugly condescending, attitude. Nothing could be further from the truth. Israel is not Yahweh's pampered pet but rather his messenger, yoked to the daunting task of being God's model of moral uprightness to the nations, and more often than not also God's scapegoat, the suffering servant who bears the burden of all people's guilt and agony.

And it is astonishing how much this chosen people, who now amount to little more than 2 percent of humanity, have contributed to the wider civilization, far beyond their proportions. We owe our weekend to the Jews (and God bless them for it). But for such a numerically tiny group, they seem inordinately blessed with a love for learning, a passion for justice, a heroic sense of endurance, and a creativity unmatched by any other single ethnic body: Sigmund Freud, Karl Marx, Albert Einstein, Benjamin Disraeli, Marc Chagall, Leonard Bernstein, Mortimer Adler, Jonas Salk—not to mention uncountable financiers, actors and entertainers, novelists, philosophers.

That conviction of pride, vocation, and security springs from one source: God's book.

## The Lord of History

Other than Confucianism, no Eastern religion has any real concern with history, but for Jews, their history is the root of their very identity. Events of their past are celebrated year after year in ritual and feast. Moreover, discounting fantastic events that outsiders would find mere extravagant legends (the ages of the patriarchs, the Red Sea parting, manna in the desert), recent sophisticated biblical studies and archaeological findings confirm that the historical content of the Hebrew Scriptures—at least in their general outlines—is reliable.

Someone (who could as well have been named Abraham as anything else) did lead a group of herders from Mesopotamia, in present-day Iraq, into the land of Canaan on the eastern shore of the Mediterranean. The story of Abraham and his people contains a divine promise that their patriarch would become a father of many nations: Israel through his son Isaac, Islam through his firstborn, Ishmael. And it also contains a covenant between God and this new seedling movement, sealed on the one side by the word of God and on the other by male circumcision. Isaac's son Jacob (whose name was changed to *Israel,* "He wrestled with God") fathered twelve sons who in turn became the patriarchs of the twelve tribes of Israel. One of those sons, Joseph, became prime steward to the pharaoh of Egypt and, in a time of terrible famine in the Near East, welcomed his brothers and their families into the lands around the Nile.

But after centuries of prosperity, the Hebrews' wealth became a temptation to the monument-hungry pharaohs, who despoiled them of their goods and herded them into slavery (a situation painfully replicated in Nazi Germany). About 1250 B.C., a Hebrew named Moses (almost surely a historical figure) united the Hebrews and—defying odds that plainly argued to divine intervention—outfaced the pharaoh and led the people out into the wilderness of Sinai. The Exodus was sociologically impossible—a ragtag group of disorganized slaves escaping the greatest empire on earth? It must have been manipulated by God, for they surely had done nothing to deserve it. It was the passover of the Lord, the exodus from bondage. In the nomadic life in the desert (no matter how long it really lasted), Moses encountered God on Mount Sinai and forged with Yahweh a second covenant in which Yahweh chose the Hebrews as his own wife, and they bound themselves to him as his chosen, sworn to him as their only God, whose Law would henceforth shape their lives. In that moment, Israel was born.

Under Joshua, they finally returned to the hill country of Abraham, where they spent several centuries struggling with the indigenous Canaanites and their Philistine neighbors along the seacoast, not merely to preserve their lands, but also to preserve their religion inviolate from the far more immediately appealing fertility gods. (If the choice was to worship an invisible Yahweh who demanded moral rectitude or to worship in rituals involving temple prostitutes and orgies, a lesser man's faith might well have been challenged.)

Finally, in about 1000 B.C., a hill chieftain named Saul united the Hebrews against their enemies and had himself anointed the first king. David, his most successful warrior, succeeded him and was in turn succeeded by his son Solomon, who extended Hebrew control from the Nile to the Euphrates and its influence far beyond that. But Solomon the Wise gradually eroded into merely Solomon the Magnificent, falling prey to the strangers' ways. Then his weak son, Rehoboam, failed to resolve antagonisms with the nine northern tribes, and the monarchy split in two. Prophets arose presaging inevitable doom if the people did not unite in the safety of the traditional ways. The customs of fertility-rite sacrifice were creeping into the animal sacrifices, and in 621 B.C., King Josiah of Judah decreed that animal sacrifice could take place only in the relative security of Solomon's temple in Jerusalem. (This decree would later have a profound effect on the manner of Jewish ritual when the temple ceased "to exist.) But one by one, the self-indulgent kinglets were gobbled up, first by the Assyrians and finally by the Babylonians.

In 587 B.C., Nebuchadnezzar of Babylon razed Jerusalem and led off nearly thirty thousand of the educated and skilled into exile, leaving only the poor among the ruins. It was the end of Israel and Judah but—remarkably—not the end of Judaism. During nearly fifty years away from home, the exiles not only yearned for freedom (many of the psalms, later passages in Isaiah) but also picked up many ideas from which their religious isolation had shielded them (the cosmology that Genesis presumes, the Zoroastrian dualism that postulates two forces, one good and the other evil). Finally, in 539 B.C. when Cyrus of Persia defeated Babylon, he sent the Hebrews back to their native land, where they solemnly rededicated themselves to the Torah (Law) and constructed a second temple in Jerusalem under the less harsh Persians.

In 164 B.C., under the Maccabees, the Hebrews achieved one hundred years of freedom, only to be overrun by the Romans in 63 B.C. In the end, after too many revolts by Zealots, the exasperated Romans decided in A.D. 73 to rid themselves of the problem by demolishing Jerusalem and its temple. For two thousand years, it could no longer be the sole center of animal sacrifice; thus, the focus of Jewish worship turned from physical sacrifice to ritual prayer and from the focal Jerusalem community to the smaller congregations around synagogues in the Diaspora, disseminated throughout the empire. There they found situations they had never encountered in Palestine, where they had been surrounded by a reassuring, homogeneous culture. Thus, the Talmud, "the second Scriptures," helped them interpret their new problems in the sure light of revelation.

Since the dispersion, the Jews have encountered centuries of prejudice and persecution, restrictions and ghettos. Why? One mindless reason is punishment by putative Christians for what they groundlessly believed to be the Jews' wanton rejection, humiliation, and execution of Christ, the Son of God. But like so many excuses that claim righteous motives, it usually masks far more complex, self-serving motives, like greed, jealousy, witless prejudice.

Over and above their alien and unsettling customs, their aloofness from "the strangers' ways" to preserve their ethnic and religious purity, Jews were and are passionately dedicated to learning, smart, hardworking, resilient, and dedicated; therefore they are usually successful in business, education, and the arts. Those qualities are rooted in the Jewish sensibility, the spirit that endured the endless sojourn in Sinai that they recall every year, the thousands of years of domination that so endeared their story to African-American slaves, and most recently the obscenity of the Holocaust. Adversity just made them stronger. Which, perversely, made them more hateful to the jealous and ignorant.

## The People of the Book

The Jewish Scriptures are the (very diverse) record of God's self-manifestations in history. For many centuries, it was their only book, a library of laws, poems, stories, history, wisdom.

The Law (Torah) is, strictly speaking, the Pentateuch, the first five books: Genesis, Exodus, Leviticus, Numbers, and Deuteronomy. It is the prescriptive insight into the Jews' understanding of themselves: the people of God. It also offers normative principles by which to judge new problems not experienced or envisioned by the original sages.

The Prophets arose during the time of the errant monarchy, through the gradual erosion of the country into the hands of others, the Exile, and the return. They picture Yahweh not (as he is often almost caricatured) as some fulminating, frustrated monarch but as a husband whose patience is rapidly running out. But the seeds of the Hebrews' downfall were sown by their own self-serving ways. Nonetheless, as Hosea shows him so poignantly, Yahweh stands outside the brothel of his beloved, Israel, always waiting to welcome her back.

The Wisdom Books (Ruth, 1 and 2 Chronicles, Ezra, Nehemiah, Esther, Job, Psalms, Proverbs, Ecclesiastes, Song of Songs, Lamentations, Daniel) encourage faithfulness and nobility of life, to strengthen the soul in its seemingly endless reversals and humiliations.

## Doctrine

There is no official, normative list of core beliefs in Judaism, like the Apostles' Creed in Christianity. The closest is the simple statement of the Shema, given earlier. To the Jew, that unique God is in no way like the icy rationalist distillation of the Greeks or the rarefied, unforthcoming Ultimate Reality of the Eastern religions. Again unlike those beliefs, Yahweh is not at all beyond moral goodness; in fact, that element is constitutive of who Yahweh is.

God is holy, complete unto himself, separate, unapproachable, utterly transcendent. Yet he is also present (the three shining presences who sat with Abraham, the angel with whom Jacob wrestled, the bush that burned without being consumed, the pillars of cloud and fire that accompanied the Hebrews through the desert, the whirlwind of Job, the Shekinah that hovered unseen over the ark of the covenant in the Holy of Holies). God is *Emmanuel,* "God with us," and even the verb *to be* has no meaning except "to be *with,*" with God and the people. Yet again, God is still so holy that no Jew dares mention his name: *Ehyeh asher ehyeh,* YHWH, Yahweh. Instead, the Jews resort to circumlocutions like "the Lord," "the Holy One," "G-d." This is significant later in Mark's Gospel when the high priest asks Jesus if he is indeed "the Messiah, the Son of the Blessed God," and Jesus replies forthrightly, "I am" (14:61–62, TEV). At which point the priest immediately rips his garment in horror at the blasphemy.

God is the Creator. Everything depends on his will not only for its very existence but also for its inbuilt purposes; his will is embedded in the way each entity is made—except for humans. The Bible is endless evidence of persnickety human beings' resistance to Yahweh's will for them, over and over sowing the seeds of their own downfall. Yet Yahweh's faithfulness forever abides, and the reminder of his will is forever encoded in the multifaceted Law.

God is partial to the downtrodden. Over and over, the prophets enjoin the people to be openhearted and openhanded with the poor, the widow, the orphan, the foreigner. And it is interesting to see the pattern in God's choice of unpromising messengers: Noah, the drunk with a quite eccentric family; Abraham and Sarah, the couple chosen to be the grandparents of Israel when they are in their nineties and barren as a pair of bricks; Moses, the man who stammers for a couple of pages trying to weasel out of his mission (far more like Don Knotts than Charlton Heston!); David, the spindly boy chosen instead of his seven Schwarzenegger brothers to bring down the giant Goliath. We must remember that this is a God who found no difficulty bringing a universe out of nothing.

God reveals himself and his will. Unlike the aloof God of other religions, this God consistently intrudes unbidden with discomfiting missions for his people: Noah, Abraham, Jacob, Joseph, Moses, Job, Jeremiah. This is a Lord who seems very restless with the status quo. A revealing insight.

God delegates stewardship of the earth to humankind by telling Adam ("the man") to name all the animals and vegetation. As we have seen, this is a remarkable freely assumed limitation on God's own omnipotence. "What are human beings, that you think of them; mere mortals, that you care for them? Yet you made them inferior only to yourself; you crowned them with glory and honor. You appointed them rulers over everything you made" (Psalm 8:4–6, TEV).

God promises all through the history of the Jews not only that they are going somewhere but also that they are ever so slowly leading all humankind ("the nations") toward fulfillment—a new era of peace, righteousness, and justice. It will be inaugurated by a superhuman hero of the line of David, the Messiah, preceded by the return of the prophet Elijah. In the Passover meal, the family leaves one door open for Elijah. The proof of this new time will be the disappearance of evil on earth and the gathering of all Jews from around the earth in Palestine. This is why the birth of the state of Israel in 1948—after nearly two millennia of uninterrupted fragmentation—seemed a miracle indeed.

## Worship

For the three major Western religions, worship is a response in gratitude for the gift of existence (creation) and for the awareness that we are precious to an infinite God (revelation). As we have seen, when King Josiah restricted animal sacrifice by priests to the Jerusalem temple and when the destruction of Jerusalem made even that impossible, the function of the sacrificial priest disappeared and devolved on lay rabbis, learned in the Law, who act as administrators of the synagogue and delegate most actual ritual functions to cantors.

The Sabbath commemorates the day the Lord rested at the end of creation, separated from the rest of the secular week. It is not merely a negative abstention from physical labor (in some cases, even lighting a fire or driving a car) but also the positive invitation to meditate on the truths of the Torah and Talmud. Circumcision makes a male a Jew, but only observance of the Sabbath makes him a good Jew.

Jewish holy days are of two types: those that challenge the believer to spiritual self-examination (Rosh Hashanah and Yom Kippur) and those that are rooted in the Mosaic story (Passover, Sukkoth, and Hanukkah, with a few others).

Rosh Hashanah (New Year's Day, two days in September or October) is an opportunity for Jews to put their spiritual life in order, to meditate on judgment and how to live a life more in conformity with the Law. For the next ten days, Jews do penance, leading to Yom Kippur (the Day of Atonement). This is a day of fasting and seeking forgiveness of those they have wronged, ending in the evening with Kol Nidre, the prayer of absolution.

In spring, Passover concludes seven days in celebration of deliverance from Egypt with the seder meal; families gather around the table, standing like the Exodus Hebrews, to eat the bitter herbs and unleavened bread that remind them of their people's harsh slavery. Sukkoth in the harvesttime is the Feast of Tents to remind them of their wandering in Sinai, dependent on God's mercy and care. Hanukkah (eight days of rededication in late December or early January) reminds them of the liberation of Israel in the time of the Maccabees and the rededication of the temple. Each day begins with the lighting of a new candle on the eight-branched menorah and concludes with the exchange of gifts.

There are three major divisions of institutionalized Judaism—Orthodox, Conservative, and Reform—ranging from the most conservative to the most liberal and arising because of different understandings of how to live as a religious Jew in a modern, pluralist world.

Judaism's rituals and disciplinary doctrines are strictly for Jews, but its ethics are meant to be universal for all believers in God. The injunctions codified in the Ten Commandments not only are taken over whole by the other two great Western traditions but also are found seeded throughout every positive philosophical and theological system in history. They show how we should rightly deal both with our Creator and with our neighbors.

The Law does not arise out of human speculation on the nature of things and thus our legitimate treatment of them.

The Law comes *from* God. His word constitutes its rightness. Therefore the Law is binding on all his creatures. Abraham was destined to be the father of many nations, not merely the Jews through Isaac and the Muslims through Ishmael. As Jeremiah said, "He is entering into judgment with all flesh."

Clarifications *(mishnah)* and interpretations *(midrash)* are later, human constructions, not the Law. The Law is revealed and definitive. Just as when God said, "Let there be light," there was—by God—light, so the foundation of the Law is precisely what God wants.

And from this primal conviction spring the other two major Western religions:

*Shema Ysroel Adonoy elohaynu Adonoy echod.*

## CHRISTIANITY

A Jewish peasant carpenter is unarguably the dominant figure in Western history; he affects even those who disdain him. His unpretentious message has overwhelmed empires, raised cathedrals, set back the boundaries of darkness and ignorance, reached out as he did to the outcasts, become the soul of a civilization. Yet in his name Christians have raped and pillaged, hounded out and tortured dissenters, smothered honest inquiry. To sneer at his significance tells more about the insensitivity of the critic than about the importance of Jesus himself.

Christianity was founded not on theory but on a composite event: the life, death, and resurrection of Jesus Christ. In this segment, we will concentrate almost exclusively on that event and its elaboration in the multifaceted Christian churches. In the next chapter, we will focus on Jesus as the personal, human revelation of God.

### The Gospels

Almost the sole sources of evidence about the life, death, and resurrection of Jesus are the four Gospels of Mark, Matthew,

Luke, and John—and they are hardly unbiased reports. They are accounts of those events written by men whose whole lives had been transformed by their belief that the protagonist of their stories was, in fact, the incarnation of the one God. Therefore, they did not see the events they describe with the same eyes as people on the spot when they occurred. Rather they saw them as they believed them really to have been: supercharged with transcendent reality and meaning. The angel chorus at Jesus' birth, for instance, is symbolic. Had the celestial throng been in the heavens over Bethlehem that night, singing their (nonexistent) lungs out, surely somebody besides a small group of shepherds would have heard them! Think of the Gospel writers' work analogously to the work of Renaissance painters: the Virgin Mary swathed in brocade, sitting in a drawing room to receive the great-winged Gabriel. Mary wore homespun and lived in a hut; God doesn't need winged hermaphrodites to carry his messages. But both the painters and the Evangelists were trying to depict what was really transpiring.

Yet the Gospel accounts are not mere fabrications. Just as with the Hebrew Scriptures, scholars can discern a quite trustworthy historical framework beneath any later incrustations and interpretations. Clustered within that matrix are parables obviously made up by Jesus to concretize his teaching, as well as stories that most nonscholars might uncritically accept as fact but that probably never literally occurred. They were made up later to do precisely the same thing Jesus did with the parables. Whether the wise men actually showed up with their fabulous gifts at Jesus' birth is hardly the point. The truth the story embodies is that Jesus came not only for poor, illiterate, Jewish shepherds but also for wealthy, learned, Gentile foreigners. Similarly, Jesus literally walking on water is not important; the point is that *Peter* "walked on the water." As long as he kept his eyes on Jesus and forgot what he believed himself capable of, he could do the impossible. Perhaps the big fisherman didn't actually walk on water, but the colossal coward of Good Friday morning did face crucifixion rather than deny his experience of the risen Jesus. It is unthinkable that if Peter, James, and John had literally experienced the Transfiguration, they could have gone back to their same old ham-headed presumptions. But the event shows the reader who Jesus' followers really believed him to be within his humanity.

Most likely, the four Evangelists didn't know Jesus personally. Rather they gathered up and edited previously existing materials and oral sources when the expected end time did not occur and the original eyewitnesses were dying out. Something similar happened to me twenty years ago when the Society of Jesus asked me to write a book on five Jesuits murdered in El Salvador, Zimbabwe, and Brazil. I'd never heard of them, but I scoured sources for months, wrote letters to Jesuits in those places, gathered audiotapes from eyewitnesses, and finally wrote the three stories and had the eyewitnesses check them for accuracy. If I were to write their stories again today, I would have access to a great deal more facts, but that was the best I could do at the time. That is the reason Matthew and Luke brought out new editions of Mark.

Both Mark and John show Jesus' first appearance on the wider scene as a disciple of the prophetic hermit John the Baptizer. As Jesus emerged from baptism in the Jordan, he suffered an overwhelming awareness of being chosen by God. Immediately after, the Spirit hurled him into the wilderness to be tested on precisely that conviction: "If you are the Son of God, turn these stones into bread." Moreover, even if the conviction were true, Jesus was tempted to use his newfound powers in self-serving ways, and he refused. Then he returned back north to Galilee and in the synagogue read from Isaiah what was to be his platform: "The Spirit of God is upon me, for he has anointed me to bring good news to the poor." His fellow villagers rejected him: "Who is this? The son of the carpenter?"

So he made his headquarters in Capernaum, a town on the edge of the Sea of Tiberias, where he chose twelve disciples and went about preaching release from the captivity of self-absorption and material goods, compassion, nonviolence, antilegalism, and most basically forgiveness, especially for those least worthy of it.

His ability to cure illnesses and his charismatic confidence gradually made him a threat to the establishment, despite his repudiation of any claim to worldly power or ambition. Officials dogged his steps, trying to trip him up on basic beliefs and matters of Jewish discipline, testing his sense of mission and its source. Finally, any fool could have seen what he was risking on a journey to Jerusalem, the center of religious power.

At first he was hailed through the streets as the Son of David (a requirement for the long-awaited Messiah). He visited the temple and in a rage cleared out the hucksters and their howling animals awaiting sacrifice. On the eve of the Passover Sabbath, he shared a final meal with his friends in an upper room in Jerusalem. The synoptic Gospels describe it as a meal of solemn farewell in which Jesus broke bread, saying, "This is my body," and shared a cup of wine, saying, "This is the cup of my blood." Later in the Garden of Gethsemane, Jesus went aside to pray, and agents of the temple broke in and arrested him. At his trial, the high priest asked, "Are you the Messiah, the Son of the Blessed God?" and Jesus replied forthrightly, "I am" (Mark 14:61–62, TEV). Instantly, the high priest tore his garment at the blasphemy, and Jesus was condemned to death.

Since Jews could not pronounce capital sentence, the elders took Jesus to the Roman procurator, Pontius Pilate. After some waffling attempts to let Jesus go, Pilate condemned him to death—not for blasphemy (for which Pilate cared nothing) but for sedition (about which he very much did)—since the same crowd that had hailed Jesus earlier in the week as "Son of David" was now screaming, "Crucify him!" The sentence was carried out by crucifixion on a hill called Skull on the Friday morning before the Sabbath could begin. The Gospels recount that Jesus hung there from three to six hours, then died. He was taken down and buried in a cave-tomb belonging to Joseph of Arimathea.

But the following Sunday after the Sabbath rest, women found the tomb empty. For the next several weeks, more and more disciples testified to experiencing the same risen Jesus. What is more impressive, a great many of them suffered imprisonment, flogging, and even death rather than deny their experience of the risen Jesus or keep silent about it.

## Teaching

Many elements of Jesus' teaching are common staples of Jewish thought, such as the great commandment: "Love God and love your neighbor." But they assume a quite different force when powered by what Jesus claimed and did. "No man has preached like this man." He even had the temerity to fine-tune the strictures of Moses himself! What's more, he claimed that the Jewish dream of a new kingdom was not just coming but was at hand, a time to begin to live—as Jesus did—confident that the kingdom had already begun to emerge into the everyday. It was not a new literal kingdom but one that was symbolic-yet-real, just as the transformation at a wedding is symbolic-yet-real. Behave as if you lived in it right now—because you do.

In Jesus' teaching, God is totally unlike the Eastern image of him, not only Father, but also *Abba,* "Daddy." He is to be feared yet trusted; before God we are all children. Jesus pictures him most clearly in the unjudgmental father of the prodigal son, who doesn't greet the runaway with a demand for a catalog of sins, much less a retaliatory penance. In fact, the father sees his son from far off because he has been on the lookout for him ever since he left. He runs to the boy (not the other way around), throws his arms around the boy *before* he can get out an apology, and gives him not a penance but a party! Even though later students of Christianity, unable to cope with unconditional love, pose a quite different, more exacting image, this is the image from Jesus himself.

Before God, we are children; before Jesus, we are his sheep. But too many well-meaning homilists have wrongly stretched that submission to cover all relationships, especially to the clergy. Jesus' doctrine and behavior belie that as well. He left no room for reticence or reserve in his followers—the crucifix alone testifies to that. He himself showed no abasement in the face of a hypocritical and misguided clergy. And he told his followers to climb to the housetops and shout the Good News. He had no intention of leaving Christianity secure in the upper room.

To get an overall sense of Jesus' teaching, one could not do better than to reread the Sermon on the Mount (Matthew 5–7): the God preached by Jesus blesses the outcasts, enjoins all human beings to shine before people, refocuses moral awareness from huge depredations like murder to more commonplace evils like anger and name-calling. He underlines the solemnity of promises, especially to spouses; he forbids revenge; and he exhorts us to love our enemies, give alms with no fanfare, forswear worry about earthly goods.

Someone once asked Gandhi, a Hindu, what he thought of Christianity, and he reportedly replied, "I think it's perfectly marvelous. I just wish someone would try it."

## The Christian Church

At the death of Jesus, his community was devastated, cringing in terror in the upper room. But within fifty days (the Jewish Pentecost) they did a superhuman turnabout, from arrant cowards who had deserted Jesus to fearless preachers who endured persecution, mockery, imprisonment. They attributed their startling conversion to their electrifying encounters with Jesus revivified and with his galvanizing Spirit. In the early years, even though they were unyielding monotheists, they seem to have given little thought to how the Father could be God and Jesus could be God and the Spirit could be God. That debate was left for later centuries. For the moment, they had more pressing concerns, like staying alive. Yet each of their deaths was a deathbed confession, testifying to their certainty of the Resurrection.

The first Christians were, quite simply, witnesses to the Resurrection, first in Palestine, where they encountered conflicts with the Orthodox Jews, then later in Jewish centers around the Mediterranean. A critical moment in their history was the miraculous conversion of Saul, a Pharisee of the Pharisees, who had made it his life's work to uproot these blasphemous renegades. Yet he testified that while he was traveling on the road to Damascus, he encountered the risen Jesus, who said to him, "I am Jesus, whom you are persecuting." Paul was convinced, and after a time of prayer and examination by the Christian elders, he was accepted as an apostle.

It is Paul, following the openness of Jesus to Gentiles, who released the church from its Jewish ghetto into the world, struggling even against Peter over the controversial issues of the Jewish dietary laws and circumcision—which pretty effectively discouraged adult male converts—arguing that it was absurd that any man or woman had to become a Jew to become a Christian.

With the destruction of Jerusalem and its temple in A.D. 73, which Christians took as a verification of Jesus' prediction of the new kingdom and a definitive break from the seedbed of Judaism, Christian refugees spread the good news of the Resurrection throughout the empire. Like the Jews of the Diaspora, no longer in a homogeneous environment, they had to rethink their understanding of Jesus' message and reconfigure it in terms understandable to outsiders, at the same time enriching it with the outsiders' differing insights. Their numbers grew, and at least by the time of Paul's later letters (ca. A.D. 58), a clear structure of bishops, priests, deacons, and deaconesses was emerging to serve their needs. Also, from the beginning until the opening of the fourth century, they endured persecution, at times intense, at times intermittent.

By the beginning of the second century, however, they also began to face internal antagonisms, drawing a distinction between the basic message (which all Christians hold, even to this day) and differing interpretations of the doctrines arising from it. Oddly, the peace afforded to the church by its recognition by Emperor Constantine in 312 not only engendered even more rapid growth into what is now known as the Catholic (universal) Church but also gave the more educated people the freedom and time to go at one another's throats over doctrines the majority could never concern themselves with. Moreover, when the church gets into bed with Caesar, there is inevitably trouble. So it has been for the last seventeen centuries.

To settle these doctrinal squabbles, Constantine summoned bishops to the first general council at Nicaea in 325 to face the problem of Arianism—the assertion that Jesus was a supernatural being but not quite human, not quite divine. Over the years, other councils faced what they believed crucial problems, but perhaps the greatest problem finally emerged into full conflict in 1054 when the patriarch of Constantinople and the pope in Rome issued full-throated excommunications of one another over the issue of the Holy Spirit: Did the Holy Spirit proceed from the Father, as the Son did (East), or from both Father and Son (West)? Over the issue of a single word, *filioque,* "and also from the Son," the church broke in two.

Today, outside the confines of theologians' studies and church officials' chanceries, the cause of such a volcanic split seems objectively trivial. Who can read the mind of God? However, as with so many other issues in the church's history, the true reasons were not matters of theology but matters of power and dominance. The simplicity of Jesus' message submerges in pettiness. Neither baptism nor holy orders nor elevation in the church hierarchy is a guarantee of virtue, objectivity, charity, or a tolerance for ambiguity.

During the misnamed Dark Ages, the sixth to eighth centuries, when successive hordes of northern barbarians invaded and subdued the Roman Empire, priests and bishops were there to take up administrative posts that disorganized illiterates were unable to control. Again, from one point of view was the advantage of respect and influence; from another, greater tangles between the gospel and self-advancement. However, missions traveled the great Roman road system to bring the gospel to the Franks, the Germans, the Britons, the Irish, the Scandinavians.

After the death of Mohammed in 632, Islam overwhelmed the Eastern Church, swept across North Africa and up into the Iberian Peninsula, and was halted at the battle of Poitiers in France by Charles Martel in 732. In 800, Charlemagne was crowned Holy Roman Emperor by the Western pope, and his devotion to the church and learning strengthened both. Since the third century, men and women had withdrawn to out-of-the-way places to purify their souls through asceticism. Gradually they gathered in monasteries, reaching beyond their own quest for fulfillment to answer the needs of the local poor and sick, carefully copying manuscripts (which many could not even read), preaching, passing on the learning of the ancients. Scholasticism, the study of the Christian truths using the insights of Greek philosophers, gradually grew and flourished until the thirteenth century, when Thomas Aquinas had pretty well mapped the entire territory.

Gradually, the church became the organizing myth of all Christendom, the matrix of doctrines and disciplines, feasts and fasts, worship and devotion that gave shape to the weeks and years. For centuries, seigneur and serf were bound into one organized, reassuring (albeit objectively unfair) system of belief— a stable, unifying ethos in which nearly everyone felt "at home." Unfortunately, this world had some quite unchristian aspects as well, like the scandals of the papacy, the peddling of indulgences and spurious relics, the Crusades, the Inquisition—all of which gave rise to the almost-inevitable need for reformation.

As with the schism between the Western and the Eastern Church, the Protestant rift was occasioned by more than religious reasons: the rise of nationalism, the emergence of the middle class as differentiated from the nobility and peasantry, the leisure afforded the well-to-do, and not least the invention of the printing press, which allowed people to disseminate ideas far more quickly than ever before. But the root question that Martin Luther thrust dramatically into this new stew of ideas was this basic question: What must one do to be saved, to be right with God? He set out on the same quest as the Buddha.

Remember we are dealing here with a church that accepted the physical existence of heaven and hell (as even reasonably well educated Christians did up to a generation ago). That belief was the center of Christian religiosity. Examine the sculpture over the doorway of any Gothic cathedral—the integrating focus as Christians entered the church: Jesus sitting in judgment with the sheep on his one hand and the goats on the other. Luther was ferociously conscious of his sinfulness, and it was clear that the corrupted church offered no true release from it. Finally, he found his answer in Paul's letter to the Romans: "He who through faith is righteous shall live." No pious works or prayers would save a soul, only grappling oneself in trust to God.

Because of the new printing press, Luther's assertions spread across all Germany within a week and found a resound-ing agreement in others just as resentful of the official church, which had become in their eyes the Antichrist. Positions on both sides hardened, the rift widened, and finally the Western Church split in two. The antagonism spread to Switzerland with John Calvin, to Scotland with John Knox, to England with Henry VIII (for less-than-religious reasons), and to Scandinavia.

Reform forces within Catholicism converged in the
Council of Trent (1545–1563), which the Protestants refused
to attend. Thus, rather than trying to work out the differences
among the groups, the council hardened and codified them.
The spirit of Pentecost that defied cultural, ethnic, and linguistic
differences was shut out. The council asserted not only the
authenticity of the Scriptures but also the church's obligation to
interpret them (Tradition). The walls were built to last. Until
Vatican II, they did.

## Doctrine

When asked their core beliefs, most Christians would answer
with the Apostles' Creed. That response makes me uneasy,
not least because I doubt that the original apostles could even
understand—much less care about—many of its assertions.
Also, many are unacceptable to otherwise worthy and even holy
Christians, like the virgin birth and the holy Catholic Church.

Still, I believe that beneath all the denominational abra-
sions, there are some nonnegotiables of Christianity. You may
deny them (as Gandhi and Albert Camus both did) and still
be an incandescently good human being, perhaps even a saint.
But you can't legitimately call yourself a Christian. At the risk
of hubris, I will offer only four.

1. Jesus is the embodiment of the Son of God. Somehow—
   who knows or cares how—God focused himself
   out of the time-and-space-free fifth dimension into
   a Nazareth carpenter.

2. Jesus/God died in order to rise and to share with us
   *(a)* the realization of our own immortality and *(b)* the
   divine aliveness (grace).

3. To incorporate ourselves into Jesus/God, we have to
   *(a)* give up the values of what St. Paul called the world

(me first) and *(b)* take on the values of what Jesus called the kingdom (them first—God and neighbor).

4. We embody that union in *(a)* a serving community and *(b)* a weekly meal.

*The Incarnation.* As we saw before, Will Rogers said, "If preachers would concentrate more on our Savior's message and less on his means of arrival and departure, we'd all be a lot better off." All the early church controversies notwithstanding, we are dealing with a God who can do anything he wants, thank you very much. Trying to fine-tune the beatific vision and the inner workings of the Trinity strikes me as about as vacuous as trying to bail out the Pacific with a contact lens. The focal question is, Does God exist? The second question is, What is God like? The Christian response is that God is triune, three in one: The Father is the Creator, the First Cause, who expresses himself, speaks his Word—his Son—who is the Logos, the plan, the Final Cause. Their fusion in love (like the two poles of a magnet) generates a third force, their feminine Spirit.

The critical question is, Was Jesus truly God? There is no doubt whatever that he claimed it. Those who assert, "Jesus was just another preeminently holy moral teacher," haven't a leg to stand on. On Palm Sunday, the people of Jerusalem cheered Jesus through the streets; the following Friday morning, that same crowd shouted, "Crucify him!" Something dramatically decisive must have caused that change. We have already seen what it was. When the high priest forthrightly challenged Jesus to say if he was "the Messiah, the Son of the Blessed God," Jesus answered just as forthrightly, "I am" (Mark 14:61–62, TEV).

There are only three options: He was a madman, like someone claiming to be Napoleon, or a charlatan working the crowds, like one or two televangelists, or what he claimed. But there is nothing in what Jesus is reported to have said and done that suggests madness; in fact, it shows him stark raving sane—saner than most of us dare to be. He earned nothing; he had no home; he depended on others' kindness for his food; he died naked. Which leaves one option.

*The Resurrection.*　St. Paul said it: "If Christ be not risen, then your faith is vain." All Christian doctrine hinges on the Resurrection. Trouble is, nobody saw it happen. The only evidence was an empty tomb witnessed by three women, then later by two male disciples, yet all of them testified to experiencing the risen Jesus. Although the tactile evidence (Thomas's probing, Jesus' eating with them several times) could well be the conviction of the early church solidifying a presence more subtle, the most suasive evidence is the utter turnabout from absolute cowardice to fearless confidence—within little more than a month and a half—that the disciples attributed to their unassailable conviction of having experienced Jesus alive. Again, somehow. But many of them went to dreadful deaths they could have evaded if only they had denied the truth.

That argument might be undercut by the more recent examples of charismatic leaders who persuaded their followers to commit suicide in Jonestown, Waco, and the Hale-Bopp cult, but these earliest Christians did not look at their deaths as suicides. They strove mightily to avoid them, meanwhile not sequestering themselves in hermetic communes like the present-day cults but living out in the world trying to rouse their neighbors to fuller lives. The testimony of Acts shows that they were in no way fanatic, except in their will to serve.

Jesus died in order to save us. Simplistic explanations (therefore the usual ones) say Jesus died to save us from sin, to assuage God's millennial anger over the sin of a (fictional) pair of nudists who fell prey to a fast-talking snake. If God was so all-fired angry with Adam and Eve, how do we explain his beginning over again with the same pair, not to mention his centuries-long faithfulness to the habitually faithless Israel? Jesus died so we could be freed, first of all, from the fear of death, from the inevitability of meaninglessness in a godless world none of us could survive. And he died so we would know that no sin—no sin—is unforgivable, that our Father loves us as helplessly as a mother loves her son on death row. Like the prodigal, we need only come home to know that we are unconditionally loved, even when we least deserve it. This is what grace means: undeserved, unconditional love. For centuries, theologians have scrambled their wits trying to explain what grace means and how we achieve it. How can we achieve something we already have or have merely to ask for? Trying to dissect the gift of grace is like staring directly into the sun rather than merely being grateful for it. The result is blindness rather than joy.

*The turnabout kingdom.*   Disdaining the material world is not restrictively a Christian doctrine, though it is still constitutive of it. All the Eastern religions we have seen are just as clear-eyed about the worldly illusions (maya) most of us fall for as the really real. Jesus put it clearly in what the Zen masters would call a *koan:* "If you want the first place, take the last place." How is that possible, unless of course one is the only runner?

Simple: Two races, each diametrically opposite from one another. One race heads for Beverly Hills, the other heads for the hill of Calvary; one seeks security, the other seeks to serve; one seeks to aggrandize the self, the other seeks to forget the self, even shortcomings. If we keep our eyes only on Jesus, we can accomplish what we had thought impossible. "I come not to be served but to serve." And Jesus demonstrated that attitude graphically in his last meeting with his friends before death: He knelt down and washed their feet.

If the gospel doesn't unnerve you, you've never really heard it. Pious preachers offer a gospel that merely consoles—the warm, fuzzy Jesus who will come and pat our woolly heads and make everything nice again. There is, indeed, a Jesus who cherishes, but there is also a Jesus who challenges: Get up on the housetops, be ready to carry a cross every day, stand up to hypocrites, and reach out to outcasts, especially the most repellent. When most Christians claim they want to live the sort of life Jesus led, they haven't read the Gospels recently.

Again, anyone can be a monument of selflessness, but unless imitation of Christ motivates it, he or she is not a Christian, just a sublime example of humanity. Jesus said it when he pictured the Last Judgment: "Whenever you did it to the least of mine, you did it to me." The good-souled humanist serves the person in need; the true Christian serves not only the person in need but also the Christ whom he or she senses beneath the disguise.

*The serving community and weekly meal.*   Service is contained in the previous section, but the solitary Christian is a contradiction. Jesus clearly gathered a group of disciples and just as clearly sent them out to serve, first in pairs and finally as a community. The Christian religion is a connection not only to God but also to one's brothers and sisters in corporate service. As St. Paul showed, that service is endlessly varied: preaching, teaching, feeding, ministering. (It is worth noting that administration is well down on his list.) Jesus' commissions are always in the plural.

Different Christian denominations may disagree on precisely what the eucharistic meal embodies. Some say it is the literal, physical presence of the Son of God; others that it is merely a symbolic reminder; still others that it is some reality between the two. Had the reformers and counterreformers been more tolerant of ambiguity and the elusiveness of divine truths, had they been able to agree that Christ is at least somehow more present in the Eucharist than elsewhere, we might still have a union of Christians, if not uniformity. But they all turned their backs, cradling their own precious beliefs to their bosoms rather than sharing their hearts and souls. Jesus must have wept.

Nonetheless, all Christian sects that have altars and some sort of physical communion agree that the Eucharist embodies the Lord's Supper and signifies everything the Last Supper meant to convey: giving thanks *(eucharistia),* praising God, sharing fellowship with believers, understanding God better through his revelation, encouraging one another to live honorable lives and to enliven others.

Those who have strayed from communal worship often ask, "Why can't I worship God alone in the woods?" My usual reply is, "Great! When was the last time you actually did it?" And why either/or? In fact, those who pray during the week find weekly worship far more invigorating than those who only spare it an hour, expecting to be zapped. Such complacent people— usually at critical human moments like marriage, birth, and death—show up and want an event sacralized in a Christian setting they otherwise have no dealings with. "I'm still a Catholic." At such times I say, perhaps heartlessly, "You're no more still a Catholic than I'm still a Boy Scout."

If the gospel doesn't unnerve you, it's quite likely that you've never really heard it.

## The Divided Body of Christ

The three major Christian churches—Catholicism, Orthodoxy, and Protestantism—all would accept, I believe, the four-part schema I proposed above (with quibbles aplenty). All three accept that Jesus Christ is both the content of the Christian message and the perfect exemplar of human response to it. No one disputes that the church we now call Catholic was the original. The crucial question is whether that original body became so irretrievably distorted that the only solution was to separate from it and start in a new form more faithful to the apostolic version.

*Catholicism.*   What most obviously separates Catholicism from the other two is the primacy of and submission to the bishop of Rome as a uniquely privileged conduit to the source of Christian revelation. Although in 1870, Vatican I accepted the doctrine of papal infallibility (only when he explicitly invokes it), popes have done that only twice, in defining the immaculate conception of Jesus' mother free from original sin and in declaring her immediate physical assumption into heaven—two doctrines for which few but the most ardent Catholics would give their lives. In actual practice, papal power is closer to authoritative teaching (which can still be questioned) than to suppression of all freedom of thought among the faithful.

Anyone of honest mind would have to confess that the Roman Catholic Church is top-heavy. When still-adherent Catholics use the words *the church,* they rarely mean what the early disciples who died for it meant. They mean the Vatican, as in "When is the church going to do something about . . . ?" Rarely, alas, do they think, "When are *we* going to do something about . . . ?" Many women, rightly, complain about their lack of significant power in the Roman Catholic Church, yet they seem to forget that by far the majority of males have no more voice than they, even the majority of ordained clerics! Still, women are precluded from confecting the sacraments, simply because—in Jesus' day—a woman would not have been accepted in that office. One remembers the prayer of Reinhold Niebuhr that twelve-step programs have adopted: "God, grant me the serenity to accept the things that can't (at least for now) be changed."

What Catholicism needs, I think, more than anything else, is a tolerance for ambiguity. What Protestantism needs, I think, is a tolerance for unity (not uniformity) and conviction.

*Orthodoxy.*   Eastern Christians believe that the church is the living Christ in the present world, the essence and source of redemptive power. They hold the same seven sacraments as Catholicism, including the belief that the elements of the Eucharist actually are transformed into the body and blood of Christ, which few Protestants accept. But the Orthodox balk at a central authority. Instead, they have a consensus of Christians in general and cope with their differences through councils. The laypeople in each congregation elect their own clergy. The patriarch of Constantinople is only the first among equals, and the churches themselves are pretty much divided along national lines. The Orthodox have a far richer sense of the Spirit working among them (and a much greater tolerance of long liturgies!) than Roman Catholics, but they do seem to lack a sense of cohesion with one another.

*Protestantism.*　The two essentials that Protestants expect from their church are preaching the Word of God and administering the sacraments, which they restrict to two: baptism and the Eucharist. They accept the bewildering array of "Protestantisms" as a necessary condition for freedom of belief. But each sect is firmly committed to individualism as opposed to a constricting collectivity monitored by overly intrusive clergy. Protestants are mainly Lutheran, Calvinist, Anglican, and Baptist, but there are about 250 other subsects. However, nondenominational worship groups are now attracting more and more Protestants.

Luther was conservative in his changes in worship and reportedly said, "I'd rather drink blood with the Romans than wine with the Zwinglians!" However, his English followers were rigorous in stripping away the "idolatrous" incrustations such as a tabernacle, crucifixes with a body, statues of saints, stained-glass windows, and ornate ceremonies. The focus of worship was the Word and the Eucharist. The Presbyterian churches originating with John Calvin of Geneva are governed by presbyters, or elders, elected from the surrounding area, and few hold for the real presence of Christ in the Eucharist. Anglicans consider themselves a bridge between Catholicism and Protestantism, with a governing structure like the Orthodox and variations in worship from High Church, which is little different from Catholicism, to Low Church, which is like the Baptists, to an array of middle-of-the-road groups that mirror the variety of other Protestant sects. Although they are also varied, many Baptists share several common beliefs. They are all evangelical and believe in the normative Bible uncluttered by doctrines elaborated since it was written. Their worship varies with the tastes of the community, from sedate prayer services to Pentecostal exuberance: speaking in tongues, jumping, shouting, dancing.

Choosing among "Christianities" must be left to the Goldilocks method: This one is too hard; this one is too soft; this one is just right.

## ISLAM

*Lailaha illallah illah Allah: Muhama durra sululah.*
"There is no God but Allah, and Mohammed is his prophet."

That statement is whispered into the ear of every newborn Muslim child, and between that moment and the time it is whispered into the ear at death, every Muslim hears it called from the minaret by the muezzin five times a day. Bearing witness, calling to mind.

Rather than a catalog of beliefs, Islam is a core conviction; the very word *Islam* means "submission, resignation," an attitude rooted in the unwavering surrender of our common father, Abraham, whose son Ishmael is the root of the Arab nations. Unlike the complexities of Eastern religions, Islam is as stark, uncluttered, and intense as the desert from which it emerged. Although the great Muslim philosophers preserved and evolved the works of Plato and Aristotle and returned them to Europe, and although a great many scholarly books have been written elaborating complicated laws, Islam is far closer in spirit to the Jewish mentality than to the Greek. And like Judaism and medieval Christianity, Islam is not simply a religion but a whole culture.

## Mohammed

Mohammed was born "of the common folk" in A.D. 571. It is interesting to note that except for Siddhartha Gautama, all the seminal leaders we have seen in this book have come from humble economic, social, and educational backgrounds hardly able to account not only for their profound insights into the relationship between God and human beings but also for the vast effect and centuries-long endurance of their messages. Which argues to a source beyond a this-worldly one.

Mohammed's father died five days after the boy's birth, his mother died when he was six, and the grandfather who then cared for him died when Mohammed was nine. Thus, the man developed a great empathy with all bereavement and suffering. He became a camel driver in caravans and at twenty-seven married a wealthy forty-year-old widow named Khadijah with whom he had four daughters who survived infancy. The marriage afforded him status and the leisure for prayer. The society in which he lived was badly in need of change, riven with tribal antagonisms and vendettas, constant eruptions of blood feud, and degradation of women, which disturbed Mohammed's soul.

At the age of forty-one, praying in a cave on Mount Hira above the city of Mecca, Mohammed was overwhelmed by a vision—just as Abraham, Moses, Samuel, Jeremiah, and Jesus were—"You are the one." He was filled with the conviction that he had been chosen by the one God to bring his people back to him. At first, Mohammed was ravaged by anguish and doubts; was this self-deception or even the work of the Evil One? For a year or two, the visions failed him, and he began to doubt his vocation. But his wife, Khadijah, believed in him, and slowly he began to share his understanding of Allah with young people, the poor, and slaves.

Once he ventured outside that secure circle, like all prophets, he encountered scorn on the one hand and indifference on the other. For twenty-three years, he preached the one God in the face of the innumerable pagan gods who embodied the very antagonisms of the people who worshiped them. He preached about the injustices of the rich against the poor, the licentiousness of the people, the frivolousness of their lives. "Can this universe be the work of a god of stone?" But his denunciation of idols began to have an effect on the tourist trade, and the threats against him escalated. Therefore, after Khadijah died in 619, Mohammed set off from Mecca on July 16, 622, with about forty followers to the city of Medina, two hundred miles to the north. It was the day of the *Hejira,* from which Muslims would forever date their calendars.

This migration began ten years of almost uninterrupted successes, culminating in 630 in Mohammed's triumphant return to Mecca. He welded together many bickering tribes (two of them Jewish) into a theocracy based on the Covenant of Medina. He was the first leader in history who guaranteed religious freedom to all creeds. He outlawed gambling, drinking, and eating pork (which in the desert heat made this-worldly sense).

From all reports, Mohammed himself was humble, affectionate, charming, thoughtful, and utterly impartial, yet he transformed into a statesman who forged a religious community with its own structure of laws and institutions that has lasted thirteen hundred years. Even so, he scorned palaces, milked his own goats, and mended his own clothes, like the Hindu Mohandas Gandhi.

Mohammed died in 632, with almost all of Arabia under his mastery. At its height, Islam controlled the northern half of Africa, all of the Near East, Afghanistan, Pakistan, and Indonesia and assimilated to its language and religion more than the Greeks ever had. Today, five hundred million people all over the world follow Mohammed's beliefs and daily revere his name.

## Doctrine

For the Muslim, the Koran (Qur'an) is the book in which there is no doubt. It is the very word of God mediated to Mohammed through the angel Gabriel, much of it in later years written down by scribes as Mohammed recited it in an ecstatic state. "Mohammed is his prophet," not the only one, but the last, the seal of the prophets, yet of the twenty-eight prophets mentioned in the Koran, eighteen are from the Hebrew Scriptures as well as John the Baptist and Jesus from the New Testament. Just as Judaism's mishnah and midrash offer later clarifications and codifications of Scripture into law, so too with Islam's *hadith* (tradition) and *sunnah* (moral customs).

*Allah.* "There is no God but Allah." There is no room for polytheism or idolatry or even pictures of anything living. The only allowable decorations are geometrical designs. Allah is unique and incomparable, thus beyond even the weak reaches of analogy. Mohammed explicitly denied the Christian Trinity; also, in contrast to the immanence of God in both the Jewish and the Christian views, Allah is utterly transcendent, in his being much more like the Ultimate Reality of Eastern religions. Thus, to put it perhaps too colloquially, prayer for the Muslim is a one-way conversation. Allah is the creator, the ruler, the judge, and all that is depends on him.

*Judgment.* The prophet won his first and then later converts by convincing them of the reality of an afterlife and therefore of the inescapable judgment of God on their moral lives. Nonetheless, every chapter of the Koran begins, "In the name of

Allah, the Compassionate, the Merciful." To whom is God merciful? To those who submit to his will, manifest in the way things are. (Thus, Islam is not a belief open to much social change.) The only peace comes from surrender to Allah's will, whatever it may be. However, it becomes difficult in some places in the Koran to harmonize the inescapable will of Allah and the undeniable human freedom to frustrate it. Therefore, some believe that before the omnipotent will of Allah, all human choices are impotent. As with the dour John Calvin, it seems that no amount of faith or good works or effort will change predestination. Moreover, the complete and abject submission of the Muslim and the peace it brings can seem to an outsider the mindless serenity achieved by the citizens of *Brave New World* or *1984,* the peace that comes when there is no need to think.

*The Five Pillars.*   Mohammed evolved the Golden Rule into definite law, the Five Pillars of Islam.

1. **The simple creed.** "There is no God but Allah, and Mohammed is his prophet." Like the Hebrew Shema, this statement is an encapsulation of many compacted doctrines without which it could not be true. This Allah, as we have seen, has much more in common with the distant Brahman and even the Hebrew Yahweh than with the Father espoused by Jesus.

2. **Daily prayer.** Prayer keeps one's life in perspective, acknowledges that God and not oneself is the center of life. This understanding is an integral part of Islam. Every believer prays five times each day: on rising, at noon, in midafternoon, after sunset, and before bed. Friday at noon, hundreds of males gather for common prayers, prostrating themselves toward Mecca, where Allah first made himself known to the people. There are no priests and no formal liturgical rites.

3. **Charity.** In a historically unprecedented move, Moham- med instituted a tax solely for the benefit of the poor: 2.5 percent of all holdings (not just income) every year.

4. **Penance.** During the month of Ramadan, a good Muslim abstains from sunup to sundown from all food and drink, even in the scorching summers of the Middle East, in order to develop discipline, dependence, humility, and an understanding of the plight of the poor.

5. **Pilgrimage.** Once in a lifetime, Muslims must travel, all in the same simple clothes, to Mecca to underline their common humanity, despite their social status, and their common belief, despite their nationality.

Islam does not appeal easily to the independently minded modern, who might be willing to yield centrality to God in some vague, nonintrusive way. Nonetheless, the sincerity and depth of Muslim belief, shamelessly and publicly expressed (even by males) all day, cannot fail to impress all but the flint-hearted. It is almost unthinkable that even the most ardent Christian would pause to pray five times a day, abstain for an entire month, and— probably least likely—surrender without complaint 2.5 percent of his or her holdings each year for the poor. Sad, but true.

## BOTH SIDES NOW

*Note to the reader: To diminish the basic discrepancy between the East's impersonal and the West's personal Ultimate Reality, in this concluding segment I will use the pronoun* it.

When we look at the religions of the world, we find all kinds of people talking about the same Entity, like different dialects of the same language. Each religion contains some ver- sion of the Golden Rule; each sees self-centeredness as the root of our troubles; each acknowledges a universal Source from which we have sprung and in relation to which our true fulfill- ment (salvation) is to be found. Each shows a willingness to sacrifice any finite concern that comes in conflict with union with that ultimate, transcendent Truth. "God lets his rain fall on the just and the unjust." Surely then, he would let his light fall on them as well.

## Existence

All of the major religions we have seen agree that the Divine exists and is utterly unique. Moreover, at the very least, whatever the Ultimate Reality is, it is to some degree knowable and yet by definition confoundingly elusive of capture in human terms. It is like other entities only in the remotest way. All agree that the Ultimate Reality is real and substantive, although they differ in the ways and degrees in which it is real.

## Connection

Whether we acknowledge it or not, there is an ontological (objectively existent) connection between the Ultimate Reality and humankind. Without its existence, our existence would be meaningless. There is a reciprocal relationship between it and us, but the *nature* of that relationship undergirds the differences between West and East. The three religions rooted in Abraham see the Ultimate Reality as our efficient cause (the creator), our formal cause (the ruler), and our final cause (the exemplar and goal); the Eastern religions see it as the absolutely pure being, in contrast to which our being is illusory.

All religions agree that the Entity on the other side of the abyss is good, benevolent, and at least in some sense supportive, despite variously viewed powers of evil. All agree that our response should be at least a respectful attitude and at best an attempt to defy the abyss and conjoin ourselves with it through prayer and/or worship. That connection is as mysterious as a long-term, loving relationship between two human beings, yet it is not a human give-and-take relationship but rather a yielding to undeserved love, in other words, grace.

## Moral Behavior

All the great religions agree that given the nature of our relationship with the Ultimate Reality, we ought to order and structure our this-worldly lives in accordance with the supernatural reality that gives them a framework of meaning. The will of the Ultimate Reality, manifest in the way things are, shows us a structure of natural laws that indicate what elements of our lives are life giving or death dealing to an immanent-transcendent union. In the face of that relationship, value takes on a meaning far more potent and real than price tags.

## Revelation

In the East, the Source is impersonal and almost beyond the concept of abstraction—yet it is in some degree detectable and knowable. For easterners, as Ward Fellows (to whom I am much indebted) put it with admirable conciseness, revelation is really a "to whom it may concern" letter. In contrast, the West sees revelation as truly interpersonal, either to the community through a prophet or to an individual soul through Person-to-person communication from a caring God.

## Salvation

All major religions agree that human beings are in need of salvation, release from the restraints of the death-dealing realities that are far more appealing than the life-giving ones. Each agrees that salvation comes about in a three-stage process: first, recognizing the soul sickness rooted in separation from the Transcendent, a state of alienation from which one must escape or be delivered; second, grasping the means by which the soul is healed of the separation; and third, experiencing the spiritual wholeness found in restoration of the sacred relationship.

The goal of salvation in the East is release from contentment with inferior reality, from a complacent failure to actuate one's own divine potential. In the West, soul sickness is willful refusal to yield center stage to the Creator; salvation heals our estrangement from the true order of things that is God's will. In the East, there is no sense of collective salvation, while community is a staple of the Western notion: the chosen people, the kingdom of God, the Islamic theocracy.

One of the strongest divergences is the means to salvation. In the East, it is very much a bootstrap operation, individualistic, without any help from above. By contrast, in the West, although we must cooperate with the Divine, in the end salvation comes as a free gift from God. Again, this is perhaps clearest in the two greatest exemplars of East and West, the Buddha and Jesus Christ. The Buddha took hold of himself, struggled might and main to find the clearest route to fulfillment, and ground away at it until he broke free. In contrast, the Jesus we see on the cross is the epitome of helpless surrender who conquered by sheer impotence.

In the end, all religions agree: There is something profoundly wrong with us, and our mission from the Ultimate Reality is to right that wrong. All religions are also in agreement—and offer multitudinous evidence—that the estrangement can indeed be healed.

# 8

---

# IF ONLY GOD
# WOULD SHOW US HOW

In the beauty of the lilies Christ was born across
    the sea,
With a glory in His bosom that transfigures you
    and me;
As He died to make men holy, let us live to make
    men free,
While God is marching on.

—JULIA WARD HOWE,
"BATTLE HYMN OF THE REPUBLIC"

To give credit to those who crucified Christ, they didn't
execute him because he was a nice, moral teacher who exhorted
us to be kindly and forgiving folk who consistently turn the
other cheek. That's just the kind of sheep that autocrats want.
His problem was that he claimed to be equal to God, the
embodiment of God, and he refused to be quiet about it. He
showed no deference due to men of pedigree and position,
resorting in public to such uncomplimentary assertions about
them as "blind guides," "hypocrites," and "whitewashed tombs."
He cleared the temple of hawkers and their animals with
nothing more than a handful of rope and his own towering
rage. He worked miracles with any means that came to hand,
including mud and spit, and with blatant disregard for other
people's swine. He faced down madmen and demons. He

149

second-guessed the great Moses. He violated the Sabbath
with seeming disdain. He clearly believed that human beings
were more important than any law, no matter what its source.
He snarled, "Get behind my back, you Satan," to his best
friend, who tried to keep him from Jerusalem and his inevitable
death. He was tempted in the end to despair, yet he hung on
with faith and hope and sheer guts.

If this man is boring, I don't know who on God's earth
could be called interesting.

It has been left to later generations, as Dorothy Sayers
said, to make Jesus a "fit pet for pale curates and pious old
ladies," no more than the consoling, cherishing Good Shepherd
who tells us, "Be not afraid," because he will (sometime) step
in and make everything right again. He has been emasculated
into Jesus meek and mild, a simpering model to offer obstreper-
ous children (especially boys). As if he never spoke out, never
dared attack, never upset anyone.

## THE REDUCTIONIST JESUS

Most of our mothers exhorted us not to judge people by their
looks, but unfortunately either they didn't say it often enough or
the inner opposition was just too strong. It takes some strength
of character not to shy away from unattractive people or those
whose exteriors suggest that they're quite likely boorish or aloof
or namby-pamby. If that repugnance prevails, there's little
likelihood we will give much attention or prolonged consideration to what the person says. That is true, I think, with Jesus—
especially with males and the young. The images we carry
uncritically in our heads are of a young man most would not
like to find was coming to dinner.

The greatest obstacles to finding out what Jesus revealed
to us about being human are surely not in the Gospels. That
would take reading and pondering, and both require effort. The

greatest obstacles are the ones that come to us without effort in third-rate church art, untruthful biblical movies, treacly homilies, and hymns that sound like lullabies.

Since there is no physical description of Jesus in the Gospels, we are free (within limits) to picture him any way we choose. Unfortunately, too many of even the greatest artists have made unsupportable choices: thin, ethereal, blue-eyed, with long, tapering fingers like a concert pianist. But the unchallengeable fact is he was a Jew and most likely a carpenter. Not too many native Israelis have blue eyes. Those who work outdoors all day have dark skin, and carpenters have thick, callused hands. What happened? The artists made Jesus the kind of physical person they wanted, that is, someone like themselves: a white European goy—the way God would have presented Jesus, had God known better.

Biblical films are as bad, depending on what aspect of Jesus the director favors. Until recently, most leaned way too far in the direction of the transcendent, otherworldly, scarcely human. Even Zefferelli's *Jesus of Nazareth* makes him like a rather chilly, withdrawn Oxford don somewhat uncomfortable slumming with all these ill-bred and rank-smelling commoners. There is no exuberance or joy in him. The films seem to deny that Jesus' enemies called him a glutton and a drunkard or that he performed his first miracle to keep a party going. Homilists and catechists too often do the same, presenting Jesus as a model for young children: meek and mild, yielding, polite, soft-spoken, and thus a man no child would look at twice. Since Vatican II, hymns have censored any aspect of the Christian call that savors of challenge and have feminized Jesus into a kind of mothering figure.

In contrast, *The Last Temptation of Christ* and *Jesus Christ Superstar* show an unrelievedly immanent, this-worldly young man who dithers and whines most of the time. It is interesting to note that in the stage version of *Jesus Christ Superstar,* the lead actor does not take a curtain call. Even in *Godspell,* there is no Resurrection, just the chorus singing, "Long Live God," as if God had an alternative. In trying to compensate for the inaccessibly perfect image of Jesus, these films make him into a quite unappealing weakling.

We have made the Lion of Judah lie down with the Lamb of God and become lamblike, unthreatening, neutered, domesticated. In struggling (rightfully) against centuries of patriarchy in the church, we have to a great extent "de-masculinized" its founder. As a result, we have taken most of the bite out of his message.

But some facts are incontrovertible, even beyond Jesus' Jewishness and trade. Jesus' sweat was as rank as his disciples', though no one probably noticed since bathing was rare for everyone. Physically, Jesus had to be robust enough to be scourged forty times with leaded whips, interrogated and mocked all night long, booted through the city, stretched on the gravel to have his wrists spiked to the crosspiece, and raised up to have his insteps nailed to the upright. He lasted from three to six hours! Difficult to imagine the holy-card Jesus enduring that. And Jesus must have had a charismatic, magnetic personality. How else to explain his approaching a group of hardhanded fishermen and convincing them to drop everything and follow him? How else to explain his riding roughshod over the temple hucksters? How else to explain his fearlessly confronting the Pharisees? It is nearly impossible to hear the words of Matthew 23 issuing from the mouth of the holy-card Jesus.

What's more, Jesus' message was *meant* to upset. His words have been worn smooth as old coins, but they are hard sayings, an inversion of some of our most ingrained values, 180 degrees from what we want or expect: Love your enemies (versus the Crusades); leave the weeds with the wheat (versus the Inquisition); when you fast, don't cover your heads with ashes (versus Ash Wednesday). We don't like to consider that the harlot and the tax collector will enter heaven before the self-righteous, that we have to stand fearlessly on the rooftops and shout the Good News, and that the one sin Jesus found unforgivable was hypocrisy—since its victims feel no need of forgiveness. However, it is difficult to think of a pastor with a leaking roof spending too much homily time on the problem a rich man might have negotiating his way through the eye of a needle.

You can also tell something of Jesus' personality by the way people reacted to him. Despite his intimidating honesty—or perhaps because of it—people still flocked to him. A toughened grafter like Zacchaeus promised on the spot to give away triple what he had extorted. A whore like Magdalene felt accepted and comfortable with him. Children seem to have flocked around him, and children can sense a phony a mile away. Even his opponents kept coming back to test him, like a finger to a loose tooth. He just couldn't be who he seemed to be. He had come to cast fire on the earth. He was intriguingly dangerous.

And this is the Christ whom Christians claim to be the model of their lives.

We have, yet again, to resort to the principle of complementarity. Jesus was both cherishing and challenging, both masculine and feminine, and most puzzlingly both fully human and fully divine—at the same time.

## Jesus' Consciousness of His Divinity

Most of us at one time must have felt a mild twinge of resentment when told we should make Jesus the model of our lives: "Hey, wait a minute. It was easy for him. He was God." There are other pretty trivial objections to the fully divine/fully human combination: When Jesus was an embryo in Mary's womb, was he running things from in there? When Joseph took him into the carpenter shop, did Jesus just pretend he didn't know fifty better ways to make a table? More seriously, if Jesus had the full use of divine knowledge, why was he so petrified in his agony in Gethsemane? With a divine perspective, couldn't he ignore the terror most people suffer when anticipating an imminent death? And finally, why did he cry out just before the end, "My God, my God, why have you abandoned me?" Was he just quoting a psalm? Worse, was he merely faking doubt and near-despair? If he was fully divine, wouldn't he know with absolute certitude that he wasn't abandoned?

To put the problem succinctly: On the one hand, if Jesus was fully divine, how could he doubt; how could he grow? On the other hand, if Jesus was fully human, how could he *not* doubt; how could he *not* grow?

Both doubting and growing more intensely human are uniquely human activities that separate us from all other entities. No rock or rutabaga or orangutan doubts or is tempted to become any better than it is. No other species suffers second thoughts, wonders if this is the wrong road, craves reassurance. No other species is tempted to despair.

The Gospel says, "Jesus *increased* in wisdom, in stature, and in favor with God and his fellow human beings." If Jesus was fully human, he must have had sexual desires, confusions, moments of self-doubt. He must have struggled with the same human questions each of us has wrestled with: Who am I, and where do I fit in?

But how? How could God learn? How could God doubt?

I found an answer that satisfies me in Paul's letter to the Philippians (2:6–11, TEV):

> He always had the nature of God,
>> but he did not think that by force he should try
>> to remain equal with God.
> Instead of this, of his own free will he gave up all
>> he had,
>> and took the nature of a servant. . . .

He was humble and walked the path of obedience all
    the way to death—
    his death on the cross.
For this reason God raised him to the highest place
    above
    and gave him the name that is greater than any
    other name.
And so, in honor of the name of Jesus
    all beings in heaven, on earth, and in the world
    below
    will fall on their knees,
and all will openly proclaim that Jesus Christ
    is Lord,
    to the glory of God the Father.

"He always had the nature of God." The Son of God never
ceased being God. That would have been impossible. Instead,
"of his own free will he gave up all he had." He freely gave
up all the perquisites inherent in the divine omnipotence and
the divine knowledge. To use a crude analogy, he became
amnesiac so that he could learn and grow just as we do. Because
of what he endured in his life, "God raised him to the highest
place above," that is, to the heavenly dignity he had momentarily forsworn. Therefore all beings in the universe "will fall on
their knees, and all will openly proclaim that Jesus Christ is
Lord"—that is, the name of Yahweh. The unspeakable: *Ehyeh
asher ehyeh.*

    Throughout his ministry, Jesus always claimed that he did
what he did, not by his own power, but by his Father working
through him. Therefore, when Mary taught Jesus how to lace
his sandals, it was news to him. He must have been a gifted boy,
as witness his conversations with the leaders when he was lost
in the temple, but his Nazareth neighbors were so nonplussed at
his claims that they threatened to stone him and threw him out
of town. "Who does he think he is? The son of the carpenter?"

When he humbly submitted himself to John for baptism, he was overpowered by the same astonishing/repellent conviction as any other human being's sense of vocation. Impossible. But after the temptations in the desert, he emerged resolved—just as Mary, without comprehending how or why, accepted her vocation. Throughout his public life, he worked with sublime confidence, not in himself, but in the One who called him.

The agony in the Garden of Gethsemane proved that, like all of us, the God-man Jesus dreaded pain and death. Finally, on the cross, he gave the same cry that so tortured the atheist-agnostic Albert Camus: "My God, my God, why have you abandoned me?" But his very last words were an act of faith: "Father, into your hands I commend my spirit."

For me, that makes Jesus the most appealing of all understandings of God: a God who was tempted, as I have been, to despair; a God who nonetheless—against all reason—surrendered to trust and hope.

I can follow a God like that, a teacher who toiled three years with chosen students twenty-four hours a day, only to have every one of them in the crunch hike up their skirts and skedaddle. One of them turned him in to the authorities; his pet denied knowing him, three times in the same night, not to a soldier with a knife at his throat, but to a waitress! After thirty-six years teaching high school boys, baptized but still pagan, I can understand that God. I can model my life after his. When I'm tempted to throw it all over, I hear God himself cry, "My God, my God, why have you abandoned me? But into your hands I commend my spirit."

## Jesus and Sinners

Unfortunately, our image of Jesus and his message have been distorted not only by popular art but also by theologians, especially moralists and canon lawyers. When we see Jesus in the Gospels dealing with lawyers (not to mention St. Paul's scorn of the Law), we wonder how Jesus would react, say, to a committed couple with children who, for clearly understandable reasons, wanted some assurance that they would have no more, or to a couple who had made a tragic mistake in their first marriages and sincerely wanted to return to the sacraments. We wonder if Jesus, who washed Judas's feet and offered him his body and blood at the Last Supper, would deny communion to a Christian whose baptism was administered by someone "unqualified." We wonder what Jesus, who made no fuss over Peter's three denials but welcomed him back, fully, after only three declarations of love, would say to those who have left the priestly ministry. Would he allow them to teach in Catholic institutions or even catechetics programs, read, serve, or distribute the Eucharist—which any other layperson can do?

Jesus never waxed wroth over a sexual sinner. In fact, sexual sins didn't seem very high on his priority list. Surely not as high as they have been in the eyes of the official church, owing to the intervention of Plato, St. Augustine, and others. Incandescent minds, but not Jesus'.

He didn't revile Peter for cowardice; he merely asked— three times—"Peter, do you love me?" Jesus didn't consider wealth a sin; he loved the rich young man, even unable to sell all; Lazarus and his family seemed comfortable; Jesus made no complaint that Zacchaeus gave away only half his ill-gotten goods; a penniless Samaritan would have been no help for the victim in the ditch; and if Joseph of Arimathea had been poor, Jesus would have gone unburied. He seemed none too cautious about observing the niceties of Sabbath or enjoying food and wine. Even "heretics" like Samaritans had gentler treatment from Jesus than they could expect from the later traditional church.

In fact, the only sinners who upset Jesus—strongly— were the clergy and the temple minions! He reacted fiercely to the hypocrisy and grandstanding of the Pharisees. And one can almost hear him grind his teeth while confronting the thick-headed materialism of his own twelve seminarians. What is common to these offenders is their refusal to see anything wrong with their suppositions, no sense of a need for repentance, since the rectitude of their convictions was unquestionable to them.

Oh, Jesus mentioned sins aplenty: fornication, theft, murder, adultery, greed, maliciousness, deceit, sensuality, envy, blasphemy, arrogance, an obtuse spirit. He was not as blasé about sin as many nominal Christians like to believe he was. But perhaps the root sin is the last in his list: an obtuse spirit, the narcissism that refuses to admit one did wrong and the inertia that finds it too much effort and embarrassment to go back to the first wrong turn and start over.

But Jesus also offered forgiveness aplenty. When Peter asked how many times we must forgive, Jesus told him, "Seventy times seven times." If God expects as much of us, we can expect at least as much of God. "I give you my word, every sin will be forgiven humankind and all the blasphemies they utter, but whoever blasphemes against the Holy Spirit will never be forgiven." Perhaps that enigmatic, sole unforgivable sin is despair, but a case could also be made for its being an obtuse spirit, impregnable even to the Spirit's movement suggesting that something is amiss and needs forgiving.

Unconditional love and forgiveness are difficult for us to comprehend. Even catechesis still opts for the economic metaphor: a God so ego-bruised by Adam and Eve that there could be no love from God until every last shekel of ransom was paid in the blood of Jesus. This view, however well intentioned, is blasphemous. God loves us helplessly. Our sins do nothing to God; their effects are in *us,* even if we refuse to see the inner decay as self-servingly as Dorian Gray.

The key—as so many Gospel parables show—is opening our eyes, submitting to the cure for our blindness. Jesus did not come to hawk guilt; he came to offer freedom. As he said in his inauguration platform in the Nazareth synagogue, he was sent to declare the year of God: unconditional amnesty for those willing to avail themselves of it (Luke 4:16–19). As the four episodes we will consider here prove conclusively, in no single case was there need to crawl, to vacuum the soul of every peccadillo, to submit to a retaliatory penance—much less "the temporal punishment due to sin" even after an all-merciful God has supposedly forgiven. Unconditional amnesty. The *only* requisite—in the moral practice of Jesus—was admitting one's need of it.

*The woman known as a sinner (Luke 7:36–50).*   Simon the Pharisee had invited Jesus to dinner, though Simon forgot or forbore the courtesy of offering his guest a greeting kiss, water to wash his feet, and oil to anoint his brow. As they dined, a woman known in the town to be a sinner entered and stood behind Jesus' couch, weeping. She wiped her tears from Jesus' feet with her hair, kissing his feet and anointing them with oil. Simon fumed. If Jesus was a prophet, he'd know what kind of woman this was. *His* rectitude was at stake, not her shame. But Jesus pointed to the woman: she, a known sinner, had done for him everything the upright Pharisee had failed to do. "I tell you why her sins are forgiven—because of her great love. Little is forgiven those whose love is small." (God, I love that last sentence!) The woman *said* nothing. No careful catalog of sins, no pleading. She merely came to Jesus and humbled herself. And all her unspoken sins were forgiven. Jesus said nothing about restitution or atonement. "Your sins are forgiven." Period.

*The adulterous woman (John 8:1–11).*   As Jesus was teaching in the temple, Pharisees brought a woman who had been caught in adultery. (Nothing was said of her consort.) They reminded Jesus that according to Mosaic law, she should be stoned, and they wanted to know what he would say. Jesus merely bent and began tracing in the dirt. When they persisted, he said, "Who-ever of you is without sin, cast the first stone." And he bent back to his puzzling tracery. Gradually, the accusers drifted away, leaving only Jesus and the woman. He finally looked up and said, "Has no one condemned you?" She replied, "No one, sir." And Jesus said, "Nor do I condemn you. You may go. But from now on, avoid this sin."

Again, no questions like the ones priests my age were taught to ask routinely: "What caused this? Are there problems in your marriage? Are there any other sins? And the sins of your past life?" No homilies, and surely no anger—only quiet acceptance and the admonition to avoid doing it again.

*The Samaritan woman (John 4:4–40).*   On a journey through Samaria, Jesus stopped at the well of Shechem and sent his disciples to the village for provisions. A Samaritan woman came to draw water and expressed surprise that he, a Jew, would ask water of a Samaritan. Jesus said, "If only you recognized God's gift and who asks for a drink, you would ask him instead and he would give you living water." Again, a matter of seeing, through mindless, centuries-old prejudice, the invitation to a freer, richer life. The woman was a Samaritan, a renegade, an outcast to an Orthodox Jew.

There was an easy, teasing banter between them, playing on the idea of the water in her well and the water that gave eternal life. When Jesus asked her to call her husband, she answered forthrightly, "I have no husband." And he replied (surely with a grin), "In fact, you have had five husbands, and the man you live with now is not your husband. What you said is true." But Jesus did not pursue her multiple sexual unions. Instead, he spoke about something more important, a time when, soon, authentic worshipers would worship the Father in Spirit and truth. At that the woman ran to gather the villagers. And when the disciples returned and begged Jesus to eat, he replied,

"I have food to eat of which you do not know." Any confessor who has set a penitent free knows that repletion.

*The prodigal's father (Luke 15:11–32).*   The clearest insight into Jesus' (and God's—and therefore our) treatment of sinners is this story. The only character in both parts is the father, the one the storyteller wanted his audience to identify with. Note the details.

When the younger son demanded "his share" of the estate, the father did not say, "What? It's my estate that I've worked a lifetime for!" Instead, he gave it, as blithely as God gives us life, without strings, unconditionally, to do with what we choose, even against the divine will.

When the boy had frittered his inheritance away and was reduced to feeding swine, he saw his mistake and headed for home, making up a memorized confession. But the father saw him a long way off and was deeply moved. This implies that the father was out there every day, hoping. And the father ran to the boy—not the other way around—threw his arms around him, and kissed him. The boy got only the first sentence of his speech out before his father hushed him. "Quick!" he cried. "Bring the finest robe and put it on him; put a ring on his finger and shoes on his feet. Kill the fatted calf. Let us eat and celebrate because my son who was dead is alive again!"

The father did not say, "I want an account of every shekel before you get back into this house!" Nothing of the shame the boy had caused him, because at that moment, the boy's shame was more important than his own. Not a penance but a party! Because the lost sheep had found his way home. The whole gospel.

But there was another son, just as blind and perhaps farther from "home" than the profligate had ever been. He found out the cause of the merriment and slumped into a sulk. But notice that again the father came out *to* the son because the son refused to come in and celebrate his brother's rebirth. The older boy could think only of what he had done for his father, forgetting that without his father, he would never have existed. Like so many, he had tried to merit the love his father had already felt for him nine months before he had ever seen the boy's face. His self-absorption had blinded him to the whole point: You can't merit what you already have.

## A MATTER OF EMPHASIS

When I was fifteen, our retreat giver read us St. Teresa's vision of her place in hell. I'm pretty sure I confessed sins I didn't even know how to perform, just to be sure. The Jesus I now know from the Gospels would, I think, have squirmed just as uncomfortably as Stephen Dedalus did through the epic disquisition on hell in *A Portrait of the Artist as a Young Man,* which owed more to Dante's and Father Arnall's fevered imaginations than to anything Jesus said or did. There is a kind of sadomasochistic delight that too many church folk (on both sides of the confessional screen) have taken in the idea of a vengeful God—a God alien to Jesus.

On the other hand, Jesus did talk of punishment. The God he pictured and embodied is not a cosmic patsy who forgives anything, even when we have no inclination to apologize. The key to Jesus' moral practice—in every case, without exception—does involve the humility to admit that we have wandered and to come home.

But of the nearly four thousand verses in the Gospels, Jesus speaks of hell in Mark only once, in Luke three times, in Matthew six times, in John not at all. He speaks of judgment in Mark only once, in Luke twice, in Matthew and John six times each. In his lengthiest consideration of judgment (Matthew 25:31–46), the crucial question pivots on none of the sins Jesus mentioned elsewhere (fornication, theft, murder, adultery, etc.)

but on the sole issue of one's sensitivity or obtuseness to the suffering of Jesus in the hungry, the thirsty, the imprisoned.

Contrast the relative rareness of Jesus' speaking about hell or judgment with the profusion of times in the Gospels when he both speaks and acts as one come to heal and to forgive, to set free, and you come away with a picture of Christian moral practice that is far different from what many Christians have come to expect.

There is no doubt that we sin. There is no doubt that we too often blithely slither off the hook and become amnesiac about our faults. But there is also no doubt that according to Jesus, being forgiven ought to be a great deal easier than we fear.

## INJUSTICE

At the risk of alienating or even angering my friends engaged in the very praiseworthy task of confronting institutional injustice, I find difficulty discovering a solid basis for it in the teaching of Jesus—except insofar as he publicly excoriated *religious* injustice. In his time, his fellow Jews suffered under a harsh Roman rule, yet he told them that if they were shanghaied into carrying Roman soldiers' baggage for a mile, they should show them up by carrying it two miles. Jews also endured bruising taxation. Jesus did not denounce the system or even its exploiters, like Zacchaeus. Unthinkably, he welcomed Levi, a tax collector, into his inner circle. The majority of his listeners struggled along the edge of destitution, but beyond urging personal generosity, he said nothing about collective means (in contrast to Mohammed). His warnings against accumulating great wealth seem motivated more by concern for the souls of the wealthy than by interest in the redistribution of their wealth.

He seems more concerned about the immaterial kingdom of God than about kingdoms of this world. Surely, if Jesus were just a fine moral teacher, one might expect him to speak more effectively about social injustice, as Mohammed, Gandhi, and Martin Luther King Jr. did. As upsetting as that might be to those who rightly crusade for faith and justice, Jesus seems to have been far more interested in the former than in the latter.

## ATONEMENT

Given what Jesus showed us about sin, I can't accept the relationship of God to humanity that I've been fed all my life. I surely can't accept the simplistic economic metaphor used to explain it: Adam and Eve (a fictional couple) incurred a debt to God so heinous that God turned his back in an almighty snit and refused to love us again until Jesus crept down and got himself crucified to atone for the debt once and for all. First, as we have seen, how do we explain Yahweh's centuries-long faithfulness to the continuously faithless Israel?

Second, this rationalist explanation shows God dealing with sin and sinners the way we would: balancing ledgers, demanding restitution, tightfistedly refusing forgiveness until the last shekel is paid. That flies directly in the face of what Jesus expected from sinners: not groveling, not carefully cataloging sins by species and numbers, not performing expiatory penance. Never. It's the bean-counter kind of minds trying to cope with unconditional love and forgiveness: total amnesty.

I can't accept that Jesus submitted to legal murder as a scapegoat to divert God's wrath from us nor that God waited like a kidnapper for a ransom to be paid, since a ransom is always paid to a hostile antagonist. I can't accept that when I baptize an infant, I am liberating someone still incapable even of bladder control from millennial guilt. As a human being, the child is sin-prone but in no real sense sinful. I am symbolically telling the child's parents that when the child sins—and she will sin—the church is there to welcome her home whenever she's ready.

I can accept a strict causal relationship between the sin of excess drinking and the punishment of ulcers. I can accept a strict causal relationship between the sin of child abuse and the punishment of having the child taken away. But I can't accept the loathsome belief that God visits the punishment for the father's sins on his children. Nor can I accept that any human sin, by Adam and Eve or whoever, or all human sin put together justifies the innocent suffering of children.

I realize that this belief seems to put me foursquare in opposition to the constant teaching of the Christian church, both Catholic and Protestant. From the very beginning, the church has taught that the action on Calvary was an expiatory sacrifice, offered to atone for the moral faults of the human race. My difficulty with explanations of atonement—going back through the consistent teaching of the church, the Fathers, and the Evangelists themselves—is that they seem posited on a God who needs to be placated, who refuses to forgive without indemnity. How can anyone, even Jesus, placate a God who by definition can't even be upset?

I dare not say I reject the doctrine of expiation, but I have enormous difficulty with it, especially since I know that Paul was wrong about both women and slavery, that Peter not only was wrong about circumcision and the dietary laws but also admitted it, and that Augustine was wrong about sex. I also know beyond doubt that the church was wrong about the Inquisition, the Crusades, and Galileo. I don't impugn Scripture or Tradition; I simply can't hold them to be unquestionably flawless. I don't deny that God is both all-good and all-powerful. I do deny that God is vindictive. The concrete moral practice of Jesus precludes that possibility.

The only way I can understand sin is in terms of a personal relationship with God. That, after all, is what religion means. And the Hebrew Scriptures consistently describe Israel's relationship to Yahweh as a covenant, a marriage. If we are honorable, then *we* feel a need to atone for our real sins—even though God doesn't demand it. We want to make amends when "I'm sorry" just doesn't seem enough—even though the injured party is completely satisfied with that. We also need to set things right within ourselves, and it helps to add to the apology a dozen roses or an invitation to dinner. God doesn't need atonement; *we* do.

Also, even if an offense is objectively negligible in itself, it gains in enormity with the dignity of the victim. What's more, consistent ingratitude to someone who's given us so much at least seems unforgivable. By analogy, how could a son who has blindly, stupidly taken leave of his humanity and been condemned to death row ever make it up to his mother? Similarly, how could we who have offended an infinitely generous Father hope to reestablish a love relationship with God again? The point, of course, is that—like the prodigal son and the three women we saw earlier—all we have to do is come home. Both the mother and the Father love us, helplessly. We can't *merit* what we already *have*. All we have to do is accept being accepted.

What helps me understand Calvary-as-atonement is that Jesus is our assurance of being worth the death of the God-man, the elder Brother who intercedes for us. I can accept Avery Dulles's idea that as head of the Mystical Body, Jesus freely undertook the burden of representing us in an infinite act of atonement, which makes certain forgiveness readily attainable, whenever we are humble enough to realize we need it. God doesn't need atonement; *we* do.

Jesus doesn't heal us. We don't just tap into Jesus and all's well again. We don't say fifteen daily rosaries without interruption and feel safe because we have a "get out of hell free" card. Jesus' sufferings are a way to healing. But we must walk it. Just as with forgiveness, healing can't work unless we freely choose to cooperate with it.

Jesus explained to the Emmaus travelers, "Was it not necessary that the Christ should suffer these things and enter into his glory?" The idea of necessity indicates that the Messiah's suffering was essential in the plan of God and that there is a connection between suffering and entering into glory. Also implied in everything the gospel and the Christian tradition hold about the Passion is that Jesus' suffering was *for* us: "This is my body, which will be broken *for* you. This is the cup of my blood. It will be shed *for* you."

The suffering of Jesus was necessary to show us in an undeniably dramatic way how to face unmerited suffering ourselves; he was an example of dignity, trust, and love—even in the face of despair. He endured his passion simply to show us *that's the way things are.* Suffering is inevitable in human life—a self-evident truth even no atheist could deny. What Calvary is saying is that there is no way to enrichment of the human soul other than through surmounting unwelcome challenges. That is the glory: the aliveness of the human soul inspirited by God, just as Jesus was, because Jesus was.

Jesus invites us to let him redeem us from our own reluctance for glory, from the rebelliousness not only of our flesh but also of our spirits, from our resentment that God is God and we are not. Precisely that reluctance, that rebelliousness, that resentment is the core of the Adam and Eve myth: "God knows in fact that on the day you eat it your eyes will be opened and you will be as gods, knowing good and evil." The hubris of Oedipus, of Lear, of Hitler. And, to be truthful, of each of us. We are not such megalomaniacs as they, but we do spend much of our thoughtful lives second-guessing God: "Why me? Why mine? Why now?"

It is the most humbling of conversions: letting God be God.

# 9

# THE EVERYDAY GOD

No! I am not Prince Hamlet, nor was meant to be;
Am an attendant lord, one that will do
To swell a progress, start a scene or two,
Advise the prince; no doubt an easy tool,
Deferential, glad to be of use,
Politic, cautious, and meticulous:
Full of high sentence, but a bit obtuse;
At times, indeed, almost ridiculous—
Almost, at times, the Fool.

—T. S. ELIOT, "THE LOVE SONG
OF J. ALFRED PRUFROCK"

Until now, we have talked about God "from the outside."
We have heard what we can learn of God by listening to others
pawing at the elephant from unresolvable, but complementary,
points of view: atheism, the numinous experiences of something
beyond, the cautious probings of science, the views from the
East and the West, the Gospels' descriptions of Jesus (rather than
the thirdhand view). So far, everything has been a "head trip."
But if God is personal, the only way God can prove himself is
the only way any other friend can prove his- or herself: meeting,
sharing, forgiving. It's time, I think, for me to prepare to
withdraw, like a good matchmaker, and let the two of you
find one another—in solitude, in people, in suffering.

## IN SOLITUDE

Prayer is a bit like sex. If we engage in it, we're rather nervous talking about it, and parents wouldn't dream of telling their children what goes on when they do it. In the case of prayer, that's sad, really, since according to Jesus, we should be praying always.

But of course prayer is also not at all like sex, since few of us find need for alibis about not engaging in sex: "I really can't find the time; I know it's important, but there are so many other things that are, well, you know: *Laborare est orare.*"

Reluctance to open up a few minutes a day to God impoverishes our lives of a realization of the genuine dimensions of those lives, but it also leaves all that preceded this chapter mere cerebral "stuff"—if it doesn't lead to a personal relationship with their subject. We all know a great deal *about* God. Probably fewer *know* God.

I trust that God knew what he was doing on Mount Sinai when he gave Moses those two tablets of the Law. Nice gimmick to focus the attention of an easily distracted audience. But the audience was so wedded to the tangible and to numbers that it focused all its attention on those two stone lists and forgot the light blazing from Moses' face, fresh from meeting God.

To know God in any way other than the academic mode, we have to approach God as we approach any other person we want to know: person-to-Person. Until then, we're doing background research for a personal interview that never takes place.

### Obstacles

The first obstacle to making prayer part of our lives is not seeing prayer as worth the trouble, but there are other obstacles as well: fearing silence and solitude, finding the time, recognizing the impracticability of prayer, and short-circuiting the calculating intelligence. We have to learn from the insights of the Eastern religions.

*Fearing silence and solitude.*   Probably never in history has there been a society so addicted to noise. Put a city person in an Iowa cornfield, and you're risking mental meltdown. Some kids tell me that if there's no one else home, they turn on the TV, the stereo, *and* the radio! What did people do when they were walking before they invented the Walkman? Is anyone truly free anymore, when the dishes are done, to read, play Monopoly, build a bookshelf—spend time with the Reason for It All? Most, I suspect, with all the freedom of iron filings before a magnet, gravitate helplessly toward the electronic baby-sitter that anesthetizes our souls.

*Finding the time.*   Finding time to pray depends on the importance we attach to praying. But those of us who will admit, however shamefacedly, "Of course praying is important but . . . ," hardly ever find a day when we can't find fifteen minutes to shower, shave or put on makeup, and dress our outer selves to face the day. (Nobody will see the inner shambles.) All of us have some kind of "fat" during the day: the commute to work or school, the mind-numbing sitcom, the phone, the guitar, the stereo. Nothing wrong with them, only with their tyranny.

*Recognizing the impracticability of prayer.*   The only time praying is practical—and thus worth consideration—is when we are in need of a handout or some answers. "But God doesn't give me what I ask for or solve my problems." We tend to forget that "No" is, in fact, an answer. Personally, I've pretty much given up on prayers of petition, since I said Mass every day for three years that my mother, who was in agony, would die, and she didn't. Nothing wrong with petitions; the Best of Us prayed in Gethsemane for release from the torment ahead of him. The difference was that Jesus knew that God wasn't going to answer his prayers. Like Mary at Cana, he was simply telling a friend there was a need. When we pour out our sorrow to a friend at a wake, we aren't expecting the friend to bring back the dead or even give us an answer. We draw strength to go on from a friend who supports us by letting us know we're not alone. God doesn't play the game for us; he just lets us know—if we allow it—that the game is played in a larger context than we're ordinarily aware of. And I sometimes wonder if when we pray for answers, we spend so much time prattling along that God must say, "Look, I'll try to suggest a few things if you'll only be quiet and listen!"

*Short-circuiting the calculating intelligence.*    Akin to uprooting that need to dominate God is the difficulty of short-circuiting the discursive intelligence that is in full gear most of our day. We add budget figures, diagnose illnesses, follow recipes, try to figure out kids, keep to schedules—all day long, clickety-clickety-click. We've got to pull ourselves off to the side of the road and find out where the hell we're going—and why. We have to open the spirit within (which the analytical intelligence can't even comprehend) and allow the Spirit of God to invade us. But that's difficult, again, because it means yielding center stage in our concerns to the One who has been center stage since before we even joined the cast. "No! I am not Prince Hamlet, nor was meant to be."

## Preparation

Zen masters can pray with their eyes open; I can't. Too many distractions. The key to praying is to find a place where you won't be too likely to be disturbed: a park, a church, a country road. Find a focus—a crucifix, a candle, a rock, or a mantra (a phrase repeated over and over)—to come back to when you're distracted. And you will be distracted. Your body gurgles; your limbs cramp; your nose itches; you suddenly remember, "I didn't call Sue!" The focus brings you back to your center.

People say they don't say the rosary anymore because "I never think of what the words mean." That's real left-brain, analytical, insight-mongering talk! The whole purpose of the prayers, repeated until the words have no meaning, is to short-circuit that calculating intelligence! None of our prayers is worth recording, but there is always a more important conversation going on underneath: "I enjoy being with you."

The Jesus Prayer is a mantra too. On the long, easy intake of breath, "Jesus, Son of David," and on the exhale, "Have mercy on me, a sinner." You could do it with any line you love: "For I, except you enthrall me, never shall be free, nor ever chaste, except you ravish me." Just being with God. Acknowledging who's who.

Loosen your tie; take off your shoes if you want. Now sit on the floor with your back against something, close your eyes, and just relax in a position where you're comfortable but still focused, not sprawled. For fifteen minutes or so, the world can get along without you. Rotate your head around your neck, and let all the tension drain down into your shoulders. Feel gravity pulling all the uptightness and the control out of your shoulders, down your back, through your seat and your legs, and into the floor. Peace. Peace.

Now take a deep breath—a really deep breath—and hold it for five counts, out for five counts, in for five counts, out for five counts. Think of all the air in the room. We use it, then pass it on, never knowing whom it has kept alive before us; we share that life-giving force. In. Out. In your imagination, go beyond the room to the envelope of air that surrounds the whole earth; you're a part of that—leaving us, crossing the Atlantic and Asia and the Pacific, and coming back to us. In. Out. As you breathe in that air, say inside the innermost room of yourself, "God, my good Friend," and as you breathe out, "Somehow you're alive in me." Say that again and again as you breathe deeply until you shed all the maya and connect to the spirit within you and to the Spirit who hovers over and within the world "with warm breast and with ah! bright wings."

It may not work the first time (too much addiction to control), but how often do we expect a first contact with a stranger suddenly to erupt into total soul union? Before beginning again, don't ask, "What's this supposed to be doing to me?" or "Am I doing this right?" Just yield; let go. Let God manipulate your soul. And, personally, I'm dead against some kind of prayer journal, measuring progress or treasuring lights. That's too much like weight lifting in front of a mirror. The focus is in the wrong place.

## The Humanizing Advantages

Many executives pay big bucks for courses in meditation with no overtly religious concern at all. What they want is to focus themselves, get in touch with what is really important in their lives, see the garbage (the maya) and reject it. There are many worthwhile effects from taking time to meditate that have no religious connection at all, and since grace builds on nature, we could start with the personal, humanizing advantages of meditation first. Here are only five: simplification, perspective, freedom, food for the soul, and wisdom.

*Simplification.*    No one would deny that life is too confusing. We live in the most complex time in history: Hurry, bustle, keep it moving, have it on my desk by yesterday. Every free moment, our senses are assaulted by billboards and ads and commercials shouting at us to buy this, buy that—or else! A hydra of conflicting expectations from spouses, peers, teachers, meter maids, kids, muggers. Comparing paychecks, clout, golf scores, youthfulness. It's like being locked in a hall of mirrors. "Leave me alone!"

OK. Here's your chance.

Each of us, at the very depths, has a human need to become a hermit at least fifteen minutes a day. Not a hermit cocooned in a Walkman. A hermit. Without an eye of peace in the hurricane of our days, we're going to be swallowed up by the storm. Whenever mothers come to confession, their penance is always "A half hour before the kids come home, kick off the

shoes, relax, and find out what's really important." No mother
ever objects.

Only for a few moments, detach yourself from everything
that fluctuates and, at rest, let all the tension, confusion, dead-
lines, and questions drain out. Merely *be* there, emptied, at
peace, receptive. As Chesterton said, poets and contemplatives
don't go mad; the solvers do. Life is an infinite sea, but solvers
try to cross the infinite sea, thus making it finite. All they
find is frustration. The poet and contemplative float easily
on the infinite sea and enjoy the view.

*Perspective.*   After seeing enough pictures of starving children
in Bosnia, Africa, Cambodia, at least the sensitive soul feels
a twinge of guilt complaining when we have tuna casserole and
broccoli again. Similarly, pulling out of the hurly-burly for a
while shows us what is really important in our lives, in others'
expectations, in all those shouting voices.

One day my friend Ed Bartley was grading *Macbeth* tests
at his desk when his little daughter came up and said, "Daddy!
Come quick! The birds!" But Ed was a man who got papers
back the next class. With hardly a look, he said, "Not now,
honey. Daddy's busy." He went on, unaware for a few moments
that she was standing next to his desk, a fat tear running down
her cheek. In that moment, he really saw her. She was more
important than *Macbeth* and "promises to keep." Wisely, he let
her lead him to the apartment window, and for ten minutes
they looked at the birds on the roof. They weren't accomplishing
anything, but something fine was happening. A numinous
moment. And three years later, Ed died.

*Freedom.*   Most of the young have a ludicrous idea that somewhere out there, totally unencumbered freedom is possible,
but by midlife we begin to suspect that anything not compulsory
is forbidden. But even Ghengis Khan was subject to the law of
gravity. He had to submit, humbly as a child, before storms and

earthquakes. Whether he wanted to or not, he had to eat and sleep, have toothaches, grow weary. There was a limit to what he could drink before passing out. If he had conquered all the world, he was still as powerless as a peasant before death.

But most of the limitations on our freedom are *self-*imposed: enslavement to others' judgments, hyperbolization of our shortcomings, and, at the root, fear. If we could just lay hold of our inner selves—beyond the power of others to warp that self-possession—we might find "the serenity to accept the things that can't be changed, the courage to change the things that can be changed, and the wisdom to know the difference."

True freedom comes from what St. Ignatius of Loyola called "detachment" or "indifference." Neither term implies that a person must become insensitive. The real meaning is "impartiality," that one seeks the freedom to do the truth, no matter what choosing the best option might cost. One chooses without possessiveness, without self-serving ambition, without impulsiveness, without greed. One counts the cost to the self later—if at all.

No one achieves real freedom until he or she can find what freedom truly means. And it doesn't mean living random lives.

*Food for the soul.*　　We are all smothered by reminders to build up our bodies—eat the right food, work out, reject drugs—and we heed them with Buddhist attention. We are also smothered with reminders to build up our minds—keep up with the professional journals, watch the stock prices, learn how to understand the kids. But there seem far fewer reminders that what differentiates us from animals is not our bodies or our brains, which they share, but our souls, which they do not. Unfed, the soul withers, and we become exactly what the reductionist philosophers say we are: rational animals, period.

It is not difficult to grasp that the human soul does in fact exist and that starving the soul is self-impoverishing, because the soul is the self, who-I-am. No one sees me; they see only my body. They can make educated guesses from what I say and do what kind of self I am, but they don't see that self. The guards in Nazi extermination camps had bodies and brains, but the reason we can call them bestial is that they had lost their souls. When I honestly fall in love, it's not the yearnings of my flesh or the calculations of my brain that say, "Yep! This is the one!" It's my soul. When I stand in awe of a snowcapped peak at dawn or Michelangelo's *David* or a baby's fist around my finger, it's not my body or my mind that says, "Gasp!" It's my soul. My intellect is intrigued; my soul is stirred. The soul is where all that's nebulous in me resides: honor, awe, loyalty, remorse, patriotism, faith, hope, and love. Oh, the soul is there, all right.

*Wisdom.* There is a difference between knowledge and wisdom, between someone who's a brain and someone to whom we bring our pain. Someone wise does know which things can't be changed and which can, and he or she is at peace with that. The wise person accepts things as they are, accepts his or her position in the universe: far better than a rock or a carrot or a pig, far less than God. Science is not God, nor is progress, nor is money, nor, most certainly, am I.

Wisdom doesn't come from suffering. If it did, animals in experimental laboratories would be wiser than all of us. Wisdom comes from suffering reflected on, accepted, assimilated. But if we are so busy doing and experiencing that we have no time for quiet reflection, then life becomes not a connected whole but a pile of beads without a string. We have to take time to withdraw from the transitory in order to discover the permanent.

## Divinization

Becoming aware that we have been divinized by Jesus Christ, invited into the Trinity family, is not the same as the self-aggrandizing divinization of Roman emperors. Rather it is a felt realization of the numinous presence of God not only all around us but also within us. God is there all the time, waiting, Atman. But, like God's forgiveness, God's will to share the divine aliveness with us can't activate until we invite it. It is the heart-stopping understanding that despite our shortcomings, despite our seeming insignificance to most of those around us, the God who dwells in unapproachable light dwells within us. As he did in a Bethlehem stable.

On the one hand, relating personally to a God vaster than the universe takes a little doing. On the other, the Ancient of Days on a throne both risks becoming an idol and flies in the face of what we know about reality. We know that God inhabits a dimension beyond the limits of time and space: God has no beard, no throne, no right hand, no genitals. Yet I still have to deal with God person-to-Person.

As we saw earlier, suppose there were a reality faster than light, so superenergized that it would be at rest, everywhere at once. Every object we see—though it appears rock-hard—is actually just another form of energy: $e = mc^2$. Couple that with all we know from religion; encounters with God are so often described as burning bushes and fiery pillars and tongues of flame. I Am is the pool of energizing existence out of which everything draws its "is," "the dearest freshness deep down things." It may not help everyone, but when I pray, I pray to a Person made of light.

The following is an adaptation of a Sufi meditation on light and God: Relax and get rid of all the "in-charge-ness"; then focus on a candle flame. Let your imagination draw a circle around it and expand the flame until it fills the whole circle. The light is like the invisible but present atoms that bond air, flame, and candle. Then slowly imagine the light swelling beyond the circle to fill the room. Then beyond the building, beyond the whole country, beyond the globe. And then beyond. Into the immeasurable Source of all light.

"The world is charged with the grandeur of God." So are you. Bow to the divine in you.

## Choice or Chance?

Prayer is essential for our children and us, not only as humans, but also as Christians. As humans, we need time to regain inner stability, time to re-collect the self—not the vague and surface "I" of everyday life but the real "I." And the solitude that prayer demands lets us face our selves without all the posturing and pretense that help us bluff our way through the day. As Christians, too, we need prayer. Without real contact with the Person about whom the theology texts speak and whom worship celebrates, no wonder the texts are no more meaningful than the insights of a dead rabbi and the liturgy no more involving than a long and tedious lunch for a Guest of Honor who never shows up.

There is not only one way or time or place to pray. Like Goldilocks, you have to try a lot of them to find which one feels best. Some find it best after work or after the dishes are done or after the late news or before bed. Some like to sit quietly; others prefer walking; still others pretzel themselves into a lotus. But the most important element is to have a focus to come back to when you're distracted.

You can pray as Ignatius taught: applying all the senses to a Gospel scene, savoring the brittle matzo and the tang of the wine, breathing the sweat, kneeling and taking the disciples' feet into your hands and washing them, feeling the texture of the skin. Then looking up and seeing that those you work with have taken the disciples' places.

But the critical difference between praying and merely clearing the mind is the connection: From the beginning of the prayer and consistently through it, be explicitly aware that Someone else is there—silent, perhaps, but there—the

God whose faithfulness and forgiveness and fondness for
us are eternal.

That sure looks to me worth finding time for.


## IN PEOPLE

My friend Mimi Kennedy was puzzled that on Easter morning
Mary Magdalene met the risen Jesus and just assumed he was
the gardener and that on the road to Emmaus, the two disciples
spent what must have been at least an hour with him and didn't
recognize him. Her epiphanal insight was that since the Resurrection, we can find Jesus only in those who seem to be strangers.

Jesus said it too, in Matthew's description of the Last
Judgment when Christ will line up the sheep on his right and
the goats on his left. He told them that the only norm for
judging whether they had led the kind of life God intended was
not, on the one hand, how often they had married or practiced
birth control nor, on the other, how large their bank balances
were or how often they had their names in the paper. No, the
norm was how they treated Jesus when he came to them hungry,
thirsty, lost, naked, sick, imprisoned. But when did they see him
in such sorry straits? Surely, they would never have passed by
the Son of God in need! But "whenever you did it to the least
of mine, you did it to me."

Some time ago, I was asked to give the homily on the first
Sunday of Advent, for which the Gospel reading was the Last
Judgment. The pastor said they usually try for "something different," so I assured him I could accommodate that. I went to the
Goodwill store, got a lot of old clothes, ripped them up, and
pinned them back together randomly. I bought clown makeup
and a bulbous red nose. With the connivance of the celebrant
and ushers, I came from the back of the church in my Emmett
Kelly outfit while the celebrant read the Gospel, lurching from
side to side of the center aisle with a bottle in my fist, trying

to cadge a quarter for a cup of coffee. I heard a woman gasp, "Harry, stop him! He's going right up to the altar!" When I got up on the dais, the priest pretended to remonstrate with me, but I gestured to the chair and said, "You just sit there, sonny. I—*hic!*—can take it from here." I went to the lectern, put down the bottle, doffed my hat and red nose, blessed myself, and said, "If you came to Mass today to find Jesus Christ, you just missed him. He came up the main aisle trying to beg a quarter for a cup of coffee. And ya wanna know something? He didn't get a nickel."

When people say they find God in others, I have no right to disbelieve them, but something perverse in me always wonders if they find God just in *nice* people. I know I at least find it easier to respond to God in attractive, charming, welcoming people than I do with types who are pushy, dried up and passionless, arrogantly ignorant, sneering, bitter.

Take the case of the panhandlers. No person reading this page hasn't been ambushed by at least a few. The standard, practical response: Divert your attention and pass them by. They're almost certainly going to spend whatever you give them on booze or drugs, right? Especially if they're disheveled and smell bad. You can almost convince yourself you're doing them a kindness by denying them help. But remember what Atticus Finch suggests in *To Kill a Mockingbird:* Get inside their skin and walk around in it awhile. How did this person get where he is now? Quite likely he wasn't always this way. Would anyone really *want* to surrender his dignity, his self-esteem, to put out his paw and beg from strangers? And looking at it from a broader perspective, what's he asking for? No more than the cost of a single phone call. And it's Jesus asking.

For a term paper in a justice course, a senior asked permission of his parents and went without showering or shaving for three days. He put on his grungiest clothes, went down to Manhattan, and hung around with people cadging change.

He made about five bucks and decided to take one of his new friends to lunch. He discovered that the guy had an M.B.A. but had overextended himself and lost it all—along with his wife and three kids—after he began drowning his sorrows in the sauce. That day fissioned that boy's cocoon and sent his horizons rocketing.

If you sincerely want to be a caring person but you're honestly afraid that this money he asks for food is really going for drugs, buy him a sandwich or a banana. If (as can happen) he sneers at that gift and really is a phony, you'll at least have proven *you're* not. The question here really isn't whether the beggar is in authentic need but whether you are authentically kind. I'd rather be bilked by nine beggars in a row than pass by the tenth who was really needy. And if you give someone a gift certificate at Christmas, do you say, "Now, be sure to buy something I'd approve of, right?" Is it a gift or a bribe to get him out of your face? Do you smile or scowl?

The first step toward the empathy that enriches both receiver and giver is to notice the needy. Granted, if you don't notice them, they are far less likely to cause you grief. But not noticing guarantees they'll never become your friends. When I walk through the corridors at school, I purposely try to fixate as many faces as I can out of the chaos of class changes. I never once have done it without seeing someone who, by his build, must be at least a junior, and I've never noticed him before. In three years! Whenever I cross the university campus, I always try to catch eyes with the people I pass and say, "Hi," and almost invariably they say, "Hi," back. A small thing, but it's a start. And it's a lot less lonely. The epistle to the Hebrews says, "Remember to welcome strangers in your homes. There were some who did that and welcomed angels without knowing it" (13:2, TEV). I'd certainly rather bear the self-defensive negation of someone's refusing eye contact than pass by a certifiable saint without so much as a nod.

Volunteering is another way to get your empathetic juices flowing. All of us know the queasy reluctance we feel visiting someone in a hospital or a nursing home, the same aversion most people feel at the outset of their first service project: "Those old people will smell, and they'll paw me and make me feel awful. Those disabled kids will drool and misunderstand me and fight me off." But I've rarely seen anyone who sincerely tried at a service project who didn't come back saying, "I went to give them something, and without my even realizing until now, they were giving *me* something. Something important." Right. A sense that you are not negligible, that you can in fact make a difference, a small difference maybe, but a meaningful one.

As for all those painful pictures of needy children, we can avert our eyes from them, refuse to notice them, but again in denying them, we are denying ourselves. UNICEF reports that each day one thousand children go blind because they have no access to twenty cents worth of vitamin A; even if they did, their parents couldn't afford it. For the cost of one compact disc, I could save sixty-five human beings from lifelong blindness! You can't crusade for all of even the worthiest causes, but to be a person of character (much less claim to be a Christian), you ought to choose just *one*.

It's not important, but it is enlightening to remember there is a difference between being humanly generous and being Christian. There is a genuine and legitimate good feeling in being kind and openhearted, but in order for it to be a Christian act, we have to see it in the context of the prayerful attitude that honestly does sense Christ lurking within the clown disguise. We have no doubt Christ is there; it's *seeing* him that takes effort.

I find it helpful to go back occasionally to the meditation mentioned before, where I take Jesus' place at the Last Supper, going from one to the next on my knees to wash their feet but populating the table with the men in my community. I look up at a kindly face and say, "Of course I'll wash your feet. It's a privilege." Then I move to the next and raise my eyes to a pinched, scornful, angry face, and inside I growl, "I'll be damned before I . . . "

It reminds me I still have a very long way to go in finding God in others.

## IN SUFFERING

One Easter, a frighteningly bright little boy named Cisco Dilg, who had been at all the Holy Week liturgies with his parents, asked me a very tough question. "Father," he said, "if God loved his Son so much, why would he make him go through such an awful death?" The only answer I had for him then is the only answer I have now: "To show us how it's done. With dignity, faith, hope, love."

Suffering here covers the spectrum, not only catastrophes from flood to cancer to the sudden jolts of accidents, betrayal, heartbreak, but also the less dramatic yet real distress provoked by what Erik Erikson called the natural crises or disequilibriums by which our bodies invite us to live larger lives than we'd planned: birth, weaning, school, adolescence, marriage, parent-hood, aging—and seeing others through those same stages.

What legitimates suffering? If there is a God, we trust that he has a purpose in it. But how do we find that purpose? How do we find value in negation? The definitive answers we yearn for don't exist; otherwise philosophers could stop pes-tering the question (and vice versa). All we can offer are clues.

No one can deny that suffering is a given. Every religion we have seen, no matter how disparate, agrees that ignoring or suppressing suffering is living an illusion, and each is predi-cated on the belief "There must be more than this." At the risk of oversimplification, the Eastern religions face that truth and exert themselves might and main to achieve a point where suffering is no longer even possible; the Western religions plunge right into suffering and try to encounter the Divine not *beyond* suffering but *within* it.

The invitation within our God-given human nature asks us to evolve—freely—from our comfortable animal self-absorption into something better. The will of God written in the progress of evolution and in the natural crises of human growth gives overwhelming evidence of a Purposer uncomfortable with the status quo: birth, weaning, and every stage onward to death. The Hebrew and Christian Scriptures, from the barred Garden of Eden to the Spirit's disruption of the security of the upper room, echo again and again with God's unwelcome invitation to come out on the road again to start over.

Even Freud (surely no believer) saw that. In evolving the pleasure principle, he showed that each individual and each culture make a fundamental choice between two options: *eros,* the life wish, or *thanatos,* the death wish. Now our culture seems at first glance head over heels in pursuit of eros and pleasure, yet it is not in the sense Freud intended eros: welcoming challenge in order to grow. Quite clearly, our society is in pursuit not of heroism but of anesthesia: the passive paradise of the womb, the painless, brainless utopia of *Brave New World.* Sex is often not a quest for love but a quest for lethe.

Even death can have a life-giving purpose. Before the reality of death, every other value lines up in proper priority. Death shows us the value of our days. Time becomes precious once we realize that it is finite and that what matters is not the number of our years but the way we use them. As Carlos Castaneda wrote, when you are in a seemingly unsolvable quandary, the only sane thing to do is "turn to your left and ask advice from your death."

But the deaths of those we love disrupt our lives only every so often. Our encounters with suffering, huge and disheartening, trivial and infuriating, dog us every day of our lives. The two most potent scriptural symbols of unmerited suffering and God's hope of our response to it are Job and Jesus, who show us that suffering makes God and our call to invite the divine aliveness into us less easily avoidable.

## Job

In a single day, sorrows engulf Job. His animals are stolen; his children are destroyed. Job tears his clothes with grief but refuses to lose faith: "Born with nothing," he sighs, "die with nothing. The Lord gives; the Lord takes away. Blessed be his name."

Then the Adversary afflicts Job's body with pustulant boils, and Job's wife, who has also borne these agonies, but without her husband's maddening, impregnable trust, comes to him and screams, "Curse God! And die!" But Job says, "If we take the happiness, must we not take the sorrow too?" And his wife deserts him.

Job sees that we can't have happiness without sorrow, that either is meaningless without the other, as inseparable as yin and yang, warmth and cold, daylight and darkness. Happiness is not a reward, and sorrow is not a punishment; each is essential to understand that the other exists. That truth is absolutely crucial.

Then three friends—Eliphaz, Bildad, and Zophar—arrive, learned in the traditions. At first hesitantly, then with the full ardor of the inflexibly single-minded, the friends begin to battle for Job's soul. For the next thirty-four chapters, the debate surges back and forth, each friend insisting that no matter how egregious, Job's sufferings must be rooted in his sinfulness. But Job stubbornly maintains his innocence. Surely if he had committed some offense requiring suffering as outrageous as this, he would *remember* it!

Job's comforters are well intentioned, like most fundamentalists, restorationists, and unbending traditionalists. At times they sound like insufferable academic prigs without the slightest tolerance for ambiguity or uncertainty, unwilling to admit limits to their understanding. Worst, they insist that their retributive

doctrine comes from God's mouth. Job is fighting to keep believing that God loves him—*against* human authority that usurps
God's mind. Thus, Job treats God at times during the debate as
if God were allied with these three: a Friend turned Enemy.

To their credit, at least his comforters show up, and they
don't knuckle under to Job's obduracy and leave him to his
wretchedness. But Job's lifelong Friend, the Lord, doesn't show
up until chapter 38. That is Job's supreme torment. In his
anguish, Job shifts from spiteful to conciliatory to bitter to defiant
to self-pitying. His fluctuations seem wild only to one never
betrayed in the depths of his soul by a friend.

At the core of the escalating to-and-fro in the Job dialogues
is the error that Job and his friends make by arguing about
the *justice* of Job's torments. What they should be looking for
is the *truth* behind them, which is quite another matter. Justice
is what ought to be; truth is what is.

Another misdirection on the part of the friends is that
they give Job clear, rational, traditional, left-brain answers
to what is, basically, not a left-brain question. What is at issue is
Job's feelings, not even primarily his physical pain, but his sense
of betrayal by the Friend he has trusted for a lifetime. Jeremiah,
chapter after chapter, echoes exactly the same keening sense
of faithlessness on the part of the One we have trusted.

But Job also makes an error of his own, more subtle than
his friends' error: He maintains his innocence *as if God were
denying it.* Job overvalues his guiltlessness, turns it into a bar-
gaining chip. To the contrary, Jesus will say, infuriatingly, "When
you have done all you have been told to do, say, 'We are merely
servants: we have done no more than our duty.'"

What Job yearns for—what the bereaved at a wake or
the patient coming out of the oncologist's office or the deserted
spouse yearns for—is not rational answers but empathy, not
only from his friends, but also from his Friend. Job feels that
God has deserted him, as Jeremiah and nearly all of us have felt

deserted. When the Friend himself faced the end on Calvary, he too cried out, "My God, my God, why have you abandoned me?"

Ultimate, absolute abandonment. Forget Dante, whose hell is at least in a sadistic way interesting. Forget Sartre, whose "No Exit" is far closer to the truth, I suspect: three people who detest one another shut up together for eternity. Even that doesn't capture the ultimate anguish: solitary exile in a featureless landscape into which Mr. Godot will never come.

*Theology and tradition.*    Job's friends depend on theology, surely no bad thing. But they depend on it exclusively: external authorities, hierarchies, dogmas, traditions. Tradition is important but insufficient without flexibility, without common sense, without heart. The comforters are utterly incapable of comprehending someone who has gone beyond conventional moral relationship; they cannot fathom love. This question of self-validation into which Job's friends steer him skews the entire mystery of suffering into a problem of justice, which the foursome debates endlessly. "He whom I must sue is the judge as well!" The odds are stacked against Job.

But that is the truth! The odds are stacked against him! Bow to that or go insane.

It's only when we yield to that humbling (for some, humiliating) truth that we can hope to be free. St. Paul said about the thorn in his flesh, "I have pleaded with the Lord three times for it to leave me, but he has said, 'My grace is enough for you; my power is at its best in weakness.'"

When we let down our facades and share with a trusted friend our fears, confusions, grief, anxieties, we haven't the slightest notion (or hope) that the friend will solve our difficulties or make them go away. All we honestly look for is a good listener, someone to share our weakness and lonely bewilderment. God is an extraordinary listener; he rarely interrupts. And his Son surely shared our weakness. Our prayer will be far more beneficial if, like Job, we look not for solutions but for a conviction that, like Helen Keller within her dark world, we are not alone. That's all anybody can reasonably hope for from prayer, I think.

Simone Weil, most likely a saint but unprepared to cross the line of baptism, wrote that affliction makes God feel more absent than a dead man. But if we stop loving God then, in the emptiness, even with an infinitesimal part of the soul, the soul "falls, even in this life, into something almost equivalent to hell."

*God's answer.*   Finally, God shows up. In a whirlwind.

It is not God's orotund words—or the whirlwind—that count; it's what the whirlwind *means* that's important. God is overwhelmingly dynamic, untamable, the *mysterium tremendum* before whom we quake not in horror but with the same humbled fascination we'd feel before unspeakable power, vibrant yet controlled, equally intimidating and intriguing. This is not the consoling Good Shepherd of our hymns and homilies and holy cards; it is not the aged benevolence enthroned on the walls behind our altars. This is "the Lord of terrible aspect" who dwells in inaccessible light, neutralized by so many simpering liturgical performances. It is this God the epistle to the Hebrews describes when it says, "It is a terrifying thing to fall into the hands of the living God!" (10:31, TEV).

The whirlwind says that you can't capture this God in static words or well-balanced formulas, whether the source is Augustine or Aquinas or even Teresa of Ávila. Analytical, rational, left-brain arguments are important, but they're only halfway home. Other people's descriptions of their encounters with this overwhelming Person are as radically incommunicable as the reasons they love their spouse. When you arrive at Job's situation, you have come to the foggy boundaries where incisive formulas must yield helplessly to metaphor, where the only trustworthy pilot is experience and gut instinct, not theory. There is only one way through to God: meeting him not in "fear of the Lord" but in awe before the unutterable. It is like drowning in light.

In the two chapters in which God first speaks to Job, there is not a single answer, only unanswerable questions: "Were you there when I made the world? If you know so much, tell me about it" (38:4, TEV). In effect, God is asking if he should check his plans with Job before he executes them. Verse after heroic verse, God questions Job about the creation, the ways of the cosmos, the provision for animals and birds, the control of the wildest beasts. He even questions Job about Behemoth (the hippopotamus) and Leviathan (the dragon), two chaotic, ugly monsters who are nonetheless part of God's creation—with no seeming purpose but to terrify. Yet God delights in them! They too are an insight into the Creator's personality. Can Job make pets of them? God can. With a majestic, patient, ironic tone, God asks how Job can debate when he is so ill equipped for it.

God's arguments are no different from what Job's friends—and even Job—have adverted to before: God's enormity places him beyond accountability to us. But it is much, much different here when Job *experiences* God's immensity, *feels* himself within a totally different, panoramic, transcendent perspective.

God's questions totally ignore Job's personal problems, yet they situate them in a far vaster framework. In the end, Job does not say, "At last! A teaching that makes sense!" He says merely, "I have seen you." He disowns his presumption and confesses that God's plans and purposes are infinitely beyond his understanding. But the dark night is over. Job has met God. They are friends again. That's more than enough. Friends puzzle one another, misunderstand one another, even betray one another. But the friendship is more important than its lack of logic.

One final note on the story itself. Twice in his monologues God makes the statement "Brace yourself like a fighter!" It seems that God not only is into order and surprise but enjoys feistiness and subservience as well. We find the same in Genesis, where Jacob wrestles until daybreak with a mysterious Stranger. Even though the Stranger has dislocated Jacob's hip, Jacob won't let him go without blessing him. The Stranger says, "You will be called 'Israel,' because you have been strong *against* God." God doesn't mind our wrestling with him—that's why God gave us minds before God gave us authorities—just as long as we don't expect to defeat God, to comprehend God, to control God.

Left-brain analysis and formulations are invaluable, but they don't go all the way. They are like the essential, but ultimately disposable, first stage of a rocket. Once we have met the One who justifies all theologies, they are no longer needed.

All "head trip" types swear fealty to Socrates, yet Socrates' fundamental assertion was that in the search for truth, we must admit before all else that we are not wise, that we must be humble before the complexities of the truth and before our own limitations. Such heady folk willingly submit to that. Then they act and pontificate as if they hadn't. Humility is what Job's friends lacked, in spades. "There are more things in heaven and earth, Horatio, than are dreamt of in your philosophy." Or your theology.

"No! I am not Prince Hamlet, nor was meant to be."

## *Jesus*

Job has a legitimate question for God: "Do you really comprehend what you're doing? You, who dwell in inaccessible light! Do you have the slightest notion how it *feels* to be bereft of everything—possessions, children, wife, respect, health, meaning, even sleep? You understand suffering the way theologians understand suffering, the way my solicitous friends understand suffering. Do you know what it is to grieve, to doubt, to yearn?" Only the sufferer understands—if *understand* is the right word. Suffering overwhelms body, mind, and soul, rendering the victim at least for a time incapable of anything more than being a victim trapped within the incomprehensible. Yet if the philosophers are right, God is the quintessence of serenity.

Jesus changed all that. While remaining fully God, Jesus was also fully human. He experienced the stink of toil, fatigue at the end of the day, irritation at being misunderstood, anger at self-righteous hypocrisy, anguish at the loss of a friend. In Jesus, God felt deserted, betrayed, condemned, scourged, cursed, spat upon, felt his body invaded by thorns, nails, filth, felt his muscles scream in agony, his lungs fill with blood, his life drain away. In Jesus, God felt death.

Jesus erased all distance between God and Job.

In Jesus, God became suffering. Not an impersonal, deist God; not some subjective God in our heads personifying goodness and love; not even the great energizing life force alive in the universe and its every cranny. But God himself was crucified, even teetered on the edge of despair with a plea exactly like Job's: "My God, my God, why have you abandoned me?"

At the outset of Jesus' passion, at the moment of his arrest, Peter—who had tried to protect his friend from suffering before—drew a sword and cut off the earlobe of the high priest's servant. But Jesus remonstrated with him again, "Put your sword back. How would the Scriptures be fulfilled that say this is the way it *must* be?" Later, on the road to Emmaus after the Resurrection, Jesus fell in with two disciples grieving over what they now believed a lost cause. "You foolish men! So slow to believe the full message of the prophets! Was it not *ordained* that the Christ should suffer and so enter into his glory?"

Of all the passages in the Hebrew Scriptures, the most obvious reference here is to the suffering-servant songs of Isaiah. If one knows the Jesus story first and only then goes back to read Isaiah, the references fairly jump off the page: "On him lies a punishment that brings us *peace,* and through his wounds we are healed." In John's description of the Last Supper, Jesus says, "I have told you all this so that you may find *peace* in me." I don't think Jesus means the peace of the unbothered, much less the peace of the utterly disinterested or the utterly dead. I think Jesus means the serenity of tightrope walkers, of long-time terminal-cancer nurses, of those who defuse unexploded land mines.

In Gethsemane, Jesus prayed three times, "My Father, if this cup cannot pass by without my drinking it, your will be done!" Just as we must, the Greatest of Us struggled with his faith, because the purpose of his suffering was shrouded even from him. But he said—as we so often say incautiously in the Lord's Prayer—"Your will be done!" And Jesus really meant it. Even if that will would be lacerating.

Jesus was betrayed by one of his own, humiliated and spat upon by ministers of his own religion, denied by his closest friend, shunted from the Roman governor to the besotted puppet Herod and back again, rejected by the people who had cheered him through the streets the previous Sunday, exchanged for a convicted terrorist, scourged with leaded whips, mocked all night and beaten and crowned with thorns by soldiers with nothing better to do, booted through the streets, stretched on the stony ground as his wrists were nailed to the crosspiece, and suspended for at least three hours. Finally, he was mocked by sadistic priests shouting, "He saved others! He cannot save himself!"

In midafternoon, he cried out in a loud voice, *"Eloi, Eloi, lema sabachthani?"* that is, "My God, my God, why have you abandoned me?" If what we said regarding Jesus' understanding of himself is true, then Jesus had reached the depth of his agony here. Had he been deluded all the time? But, just as at the agony in Gethsemane, Jesus pleaded his cause but then yielded to God's will. Luke says, "Jesus cried out in a loud voice, 'Father, into your hands I commit my spirit.' With these words, he breathed his last." Surrender. Without surety but with trust.

As George Macdonald wrote, "The Son of God suffered unto death, not that men might not suffer, but that their sufferings might be like his."

Remember the passage from Philippians about Jesus' incarnation: He emptied himself, gave up all he had, not in obedience, as so many theologians say. No, in trusting love. Obedience is of the will; love is of the heart. As Christ was witness on the cross to utter trust in God, so we too are called—if we claim Christ as our model—to empty ourselves and become empowered by our emptiness. As the Hindu verse says, "When you are hollowed out, then you will be full."

God answered Job from the wild whirlwind; Jesus answers us from the impotence of the cross. Put the question of your agony, doubt, bewilderment to Jesus. But don't go for your answer to Jesus quietly preaching the Sermon on the Mount. Don't go to Jesus riding triumphantly on Palm Sunday. Go only to Jesus hanging on the cross. He can answer you only from there.

## The Attitude You Should Have

As a preface to his declaration about the Incarnation in Philippians, St. Paul said, "The attitude you should have is the one that Christ Jesus had."

Wisdom is making peace with the unchangeable. We have the freedom to face the unavoidable with dignity, to understand the transformational value that attitude works on suffering. Viktor Frankl wrote that in concentration camps, "what alone remains is 'the last of human freedoms'—the ability to choose one's attitude in a given set of circumstances." What Frankl asked is not optimism in the face of pessimism but hope in the face of hopelessness.

Are we responsible for our unmerited suffering? The answer is no. And yes. We are not responsible for our predicament as its cause—whether it be cancer or job loss or the death of a child or spouse. But we are responsible for what we do with the effects, for what we build from the rubble that fate has made of our lives.

One of the greatest souls I've ever been privileged to know was a fortyish merchant seaman with the improbable name Bill Fold, whom I met while I was a weekend chaplain at a cancer hospital. Not only was Bill dying of cancer, but he had contracted tuberculosis and had to be kept in isolation. On top of that, he had had a laryngectomy and communicated only on one of those black-backed pads where the writing disappears when you lift the wax paper. One day, gowned and masked, I said, "Bill, sometimes it must be very lonely." He gave a small smile and wrote on his pad, "Yes. But isn't it wonderful that God trusts me enough to give it to me?"

Ah!

That doomed seafarer, without benefit or bane of advanced schooling, the great books, years of philosophy and theology, in the crucible of his soul had laid hold of what the great Dostoyevsky discovered: "There is only one thing I dread: not to be worthy of my sufferings."

"Be still and know that I am God."

# BIBLIOGRAPHY

Adler, Mortimer J. *How to Think about God: A Guide for the Twentieth-Century Pagan.* New York: Macmillan, 1980.

Arendt, Hannah. *The Human Condition.* Chicago: University of Chicago Press, 1958.

Bergson, Henri. *The Two Sources of Morality and Religion.* Translated by R. Ashley Audra and Cloudesley Brereton, with the assistance of W. Horsfall Carter. New York: Henry Holt, 1935.

Bettelheim, Bruno. "Freud and the Soul." *The New Yorker,* 1 March 1982.

Campbell, Joseph, and Bill Moyers. *The Power of Myth.* Edited by Betty Sue Flowers. New York: Doubleday, 1988.

Capra, Fritzof. "The Tao of Physics." *Saturday Review,* 10 December 1977.

Donceel, Joseph F. *The Searching Mind: An Introduction to a Philosophy of God.* Notre Dame, Ind.: University of Notre Dame Press, 1979.

Eliade, Mircea. *The Sacred and the Profane: The Nature of Religion.* Translated by Willard R. Trask. New York: Harcourt Brace, 1959.

Erikson, Erik H. *Identity and the Life Cycle.* New York: Norton, 1980.

Fellows, Ward J. *Religions East and West.* New York: Holt, Rinehart, and Winston, 1979.

Ferguson, Kitty. *The Fire in the Equations: Science, Religion, and the Search for God.* Grand Rapids, Mich.: William B. Eerdmans, 1995.

Frankl, Viktor Emil. *Man's Search for Meaning: An Introduction to Logotherapy.* Translated by Ilse Lasch. Boston: Beacon Press, 1963.

Gellman, Marc, and Thomas Hartman. *Where Does God Live?* New York: Triumph Books, 1991.

"God Decentralized." *New York Times Magazine,* 7 December 1997.

Goleman, Daniel. "Back from the Brink." *Psychology Today,* April 1997.

Heschel, Abraham J. *Who Is Man?* Stanford, Calif.: Stanford University Press, 1965.

Hitchcock, James. *The Recovery of the Sacred.* New York: Seabury Press, 1974.

James, William. *The Varieties of Religious Experience: A Study in Human Nature.* New York: Longmans, Green, 1902.

Jung, Carl Gustav. *Psychology and Religion.* New Haven, Conn.: Yale University Press, 1938.

Kelsey, Morton T. *Companions on the Inner Way: The Art of Spiritual Guidance.* New York: Crossroad, 1983.

Koestler, Arthur. "Cosmic Consciousness." *Psychology Today,* April 1977.

Kreeft, Peter. *Making Sense out of Suffering.* Ann Arbor, Mich.: Servant, 1986.

Lasch, Christopher. *The Culture of Narcissism: American Life in an Age of Diminishing Expectations.* New York: Norton, 1978.

Lewis, C. S. *The Abolition of Man; or, Reflections on Education with Special Reference to the Teaching of English in the Upper Forms of Schools.* New York: Macmillan, 1947.

———. *The Problem of Pain.* New York: Macmillan, 1962.

Liderbach, Daniel. *The Numinous Universe.* New York: Paulist Press, 1989.

Martin, James, ed. *How Can I Find God? The Famous and the Not-So-Famous Consider the Quintessential Question.* Liguori, Mo.: Triumph Books, 1997.

Maslow, Abraham H. *The Farther Reaches of Human Nature.* New York: Viking Press, 1971.

Moreland, J. P., and Kai Nielsen. *Does God Exist? The Debate between Theists and Atheists.* Buffalo, N.Y.: Prometheus Books, 1993.

Nash, Madeleine. "How Did Life Begin?" *Time,* 11 October 1993.

Niebuhr, Reinhold. *The Godly and Ungodly.* London: Faber and Faber, 1959.

———. *Human Nature.* Englewood Cliffs, N.J.: Prentice Hall, 1964.

Otto, Rudolf. *The Idea of the Holy: An Inquiry into the Non-rational Factor in the Idea of the Divine and Its Relation to the Rational.* Translated by John W. Harvey. London: Oxford University Press, 1923.

Peck, M. Scott. *The Road Less Traveled: A New Psychology of Love, Traditional Values, and Spiritual Growth.* New York: Simon and Schuster, 1978.

Pippard, Brian. "The Invincible Ignorance of Science." *Contemporary Physics* 29 (1997).

Rosenfeld, Albert. "When Man Becomes God." *Saturday Review,* 10 December 1977.

Sagan, Carl. *Cosmos.* New York: Random House, 1980.

———. *The Dragons of Eden: Speculations on the Evolution of Human Intelligence.* New York: Random House, 1977.

Smith, Huston. *The Religions of Man.* New York: Harper, 1958.

Smith, Wilfred Cantwell. *Patterns of Faith around the World.* New York: Harper, 1958.

Stephens, G. Lynn, and Gregory Pence. *Seven Dilemmas in World Religions.* New York: Paragon House, 1994.

Tillich, Paul. *Christianity and the Encounter of the World Religions.* New York: Columbia University Press, 1963.

Verhalen, Philip A. *Faith in a Secularized World.* New York: Paulist Press, 1976.

Weil, Simone. *Waiting for God.* Translated by Emma Gruafurd. New York: Putnam, 1951.

Woodward, Kenneth. "2,000 Years of Jesus." *Newsweek,* 29 March 1999.